SPIRIT COMMUNICATIONS

A BOOK

WRITTEN BY THE

SPIRITS OF THE SO-CALLED DEAD,

WITH THEIR OWN MATERIALIZED HANDS, BY THE PROCESS OF INDEPENDENT SLATE-WRITING,

THROUGH

MRS. LIZZIE S. GREEN AND OTHERS,

AS MEDIUMS.

COMPILED AND ARRANGED BY
C. G. HELLEBERG,

Life is real! life is earnest!
And the grave is not its goal.
Dust thou art, to dust returnest,
Was not written of the soul.
—Longfellow.

SPIRIT COMMUNICATIONS.

CHAPTER I.

INTRODUCTION.

The communications in this little volume, purporting to come from disembodied spirits, came in the manner hereinafter stated, and all that I had to do with them was to faithfully and to the letter transcribe them from the slate on which they were written into blank memorandum books which I procured for the purpose. Before laying before the reader the *modus operandi* of their delivery, I deem it proper that I should give a brief outline of my own history, especially do I feel the importance of this since I am little known outside of the circle of my immediate acquaintances. It has always been my aim in life to live uprightly before God and man, and as to the success of this noble purpose, formed in early life, I may confidently refer to my neighbors, and many of the leading citizens of Cincinnati, Ohio, with whom I have enjoyed an intimate social and business acquaintance for nearly forty years. I do not know why I should have been made the recipient and custodian of the truly remarkable spirit communications contained in the following pages, except from a long lifetime of honest endeavor to do right I was deemed worthy, and from the additional consideration that the spirits interested in the work knew I would cordially co-operate with them in laying the matter presented before the world, and that, happily, I possessed the pecuniary means to do so.

I was born at Grafriset, near Fahlun, in the kingdom of Sweden, March 1, 1811, and have now passed my seventy-first year. At the age of sixteen I entered the Swedish army, and at nineteen became a student at Upsala University, where I remained for two years.

After rendering military service for five years, and passing a successful examination, I was permitted to enter the civil service of my country. In the capacity of land surveyor I served for over ten years, when a desire to personally witness the workings of republican institutions induced me to make an application to travel in foreign countries, which permission I obtained for the period of two years. In 1844 I left my native land for the United States, and in 1845 located at Cincinnati, Ohio, and soon thereafter engaged in the art of daguerreotyping, and afterwards photographing, and in the following year married Miss Annie E. Franks, daughter of Frederick Franks, a leading and influential citizen of the city, who is still remembered as the proprietor of Cincinnati's early famous museum. In religion I was raised a Lutheran, but at the time (1879) of embracing spiritualism and for thirty years preceding I was a devout and earnest Swedenborgian. I commenced the investigation of spiritual phenomena in 1879, and soon became convinced of the sublime truths of the spiritual philosophy.

As in the following pages the exalted spirit of Madam Fredrika Ehrenborg imparts, among other things, marvelous information in regard to the Planet Mars, of our solar system, it is deemed fitting that somewhat of her history should be made known in this connection:

She was born March 15, 1794, in the Province of Wermland, in the kingdom of Sweden, and at the age of seventeen married a highly esteemed nobleman, Casper Isac Michael Ehrenborg. He left the body in 1823, and was at the time Chief Justice of Sweden. Madam Ehrenborg was an enthusiastic Swedenborgian, and she passed to the higher life in the Swedish city of Linköping on the 20th of May, 1873. Her life in many respects was an eventful one, and largely devoted to literary pursuits. She translated writings on religious subjects from several languages into Swedish, and wrote books and pamphlets in the interest of Swedenborgianism, and visited England, Switzerland, Denmark,

Germany and France in search of materials for her works. It was not my good fortune to have met this eminent lady during her mortal life, but I happily enjoyed a truly instructive and pleasant correspondence with her during the last three years of her life in the form.

I commenced my investigations in September, 1881, with the celebrated medium Mrs. Lizzie S. Green, through whose mediumship most of the communications to follow were written. For ten months I had never less than two sittings a week, and the largest portion of that time four per week, and have had ample opportunities to study her true character. As the result I am justified by the truth in proclaiming to the world my thorough conviction of her honesty, purity and simplicity of character. Her education, as I have been informed, was sadly neglected in youth, and she has had few opportunities to improve in later years. She married the Hon. Edward H. Green, of Aurora, Indiana, before her eighteenth year, and has devoted her succeeding years until recently to the domestic duties of life and to the raising of a family, of whom only one, a daughter, survives. Her husband served with ability a numerous and intelligent constituency in the Indiana legislature of 1866-7, and served recently and to general acceptance two terms of two years each as Mayor of Aurora, Indiana, his native city.

The communications of spirits contained in this volume were written by the spirits with their own materialized hands, and the process was generally as follows: A small stand of the ordinary kind in construction, covered by a table cloth, was used, the medium placing with one hand under the covering of the stand a slate on which was placed a small piece of pencil. The other hand of the medium was continually exposed to full view, as was also her entire form. Both double and single slates were used. We heard the writing as it progressed, and when the slate was filled it would be indicated by distinct taps on the slate and the dropping of the pencil. The slate would be then taken out, and as the chosen scribe I would faithfully transcribe the written matter into the book aforementioned, and the slate would then be cleaned and returned under the stand, and in this manner all the matter hereinafter set forth was produced. I have reported it *verbatim et literatim*, without changing it in the slightest degree, neither adding nor taking therefrom a single word. Each sitting would occupy from one to two hours, and in broad daylight. I have taken occasion to preface some of these communications with a few lines, by way of explanation and to secure clearness of understanding in relation to them.

This volume is truly a book written by the spirits themselves, and whatever merit it may possess, they alone are entitled to the credit, and whatever of demerit, if any, they alone are chargeable and responsible. Of one thing both the mediums and myself can truly avouch, and are willing to solemnize with our oaths, namely, that we had nothing whatever to do with the production of the communications except so far as we may have aided the communicating intelligences by furnishing them with the necessary and required conditions.

I launch forth the work not, however, without misgivings as to its reception and fate in this age of incredulity and skepticism, and my only hope is that it may be instrumental in doing good, if but only in a feeble degree, which alone will be ample compensation for my time and labor.

Carl Gustaf Helleberg.

177 Auburn street, Cincinnati, Ohio.

CHAPTER II.

My investigations of spiritualism commenced with the excellent medium, Mrs. Laura Mosser, now Mrs. Carter, through whose mediumship I had the first slate-writing, August 31, 1879, at her residence, No. 253 Laurel street, Cincinnati, Ohio, from my spirit friend, William Gailard, and my dear son Emil. My truth-loving friend, Mr. S. G. Anderson, at my request, introduced me to Mrs. Mosser, at her residence, where we both on a clear Sunday morning, after we had some communications between a double slate from Mr. Gailard and my son, saw a spirit hand between us, into which Mr. Anderson put his handkerchief, which was taken under the stand, and afterwards came out tied in three knots. It was written on the slate at the same time that Mr. Anderson's two sisters and his brother John, who all many years ago had passed away in Sweden, each of them had tied a knot. During this occurrence we had Mrs. Mosser in full view, who was rocking in a rocking chair, and the only part hidden was her right hand when it held the slate under the small stand. From this remarkable result I concluded to go on with the investigation, and had many interesting communications, mostly concerning family relations, until the 8th of December, 1880, when I became acquainted with that most respectable lady, Mrs. Annie Cooper, who is a true and honest medium. Through her gifts I had many wonderful manifestations, consisting of slate-writings and materializations, etc. I will mention only a few. On the 11th May, 1881, among other things which appeared on the slate was the following:

"Good morning, my dear friend. Across the deep I have communicated to you. With great pleasure I accept the opportunity of still doing so. I am anxious that all I hold dear should understand this phenomenon. Hope lingers around me that I shall be able to make myself known as if on earth. One thing I thank you for, the kind appreciation of a small tribute of friendship I tried to bestow. Every day since I came here I have learned something. Knowledge is not stopped by the change. My friend, many persons think that when the change called death comes and the spirit is released from the body, it becomes perfect at once. That is a mistake; we come out of the earthly body with all the propensities which actuate us while in it, and we come out of them only as we are educated and progress. Oh, dear friend, I can see now that there are many human beings dazed at the wiles of mistakes made by early education, instead of looking up to something higher and brighter. Yes, man still asks, with prayerful heart, what are his wants to be in the future? and why was he born? and why does he die? Oh, why does man mourn over a law that was ordained for the benefit of all mankind? Why tears fall when he stands where the form of some loved one is laid? Is hope gone? Yes, because they know not where they are gone and what they are now. No one should mourn at death, for death is as legitimate as birth. Yes, no science, with all its bright knowledge, has been able to penetrate this system or sphere peopled by those who once dwelt as you do now. Oh, if suffering humanity could realize these beautiful truths, it would remove every doubt and dispel every fear that death transports man far away from earthly loved ones. My dear friend, to you this knowledge has been like a gentle zephyr that cools the cheeks on a warm summer evening. I am happy to be able to see you in possession of these noble sentiments. Let eternal progression be engraved on your banner and you will soar far above doubt and mystery, that surround so many in earth life. Man no longer bows to an angry God, nor needs a mediator to propitiate him. I am so happy to be able now to enjoy and fully realize what I believed to be true, with but little besides my own evidence and knowledge to convince me that it was a truth. I have been reproved even for an acknowledgment, but all do not understand alike. I was fully assured before my spirit left the physical habitation for spiritual inheritance that I was surrounded by angels, kind and loving, guarding and guiding me to a higher and better life. I passed through as if in a gentle slumber, awakening to meet many bright faces, yes, too many to number, that had gone before and landed safely on the bright, celestial shore. Earthly views can not comprehend heavenly joys.

Oh, think of it, my friend, to meet those to whom you are bound to by the ties of nature in early affection, never, never to part again, but to dwell in the light of a harmonious atmosphere of love, surrounded by angels and music from the bright realms above. There is no end to life, the spirit is eternal, and as we travel onward we can look upward in hope, for there is always something above. I will be able to communicate to you on different subjects the next interview. Give my love to your dear lady. I will now call on her, and we will yet meet, but not as strangers. In the language of flowers, we remember in the sweet forget me not.[1] Adieu for the present. Your most sincere friend,

"Fredrika Ehrenborg."

This was the first communication between the double slate from Madam Ehrenborg, and on the 19th of May she gave another one, as follows:

"Good morning, my dear friend. In love and justice for your kindness I come this morning. I feel like writing on that subject, justice, for it enters into the divine unfolding of eternity. Millions stand at the bar of the great tribune waiting to hear their sentence pronounced. Justice enters into the majesty of universal law. What generation can gather it and hold it in their embrace? Yes, justice is the universal law, that no age, no nation can control or hold in subjection. When they have gained one step in the right direction they may then think they have gained it all, but as we ascend the steps to that mighty throne of infinity we see justice beyond the ken of hundreds of humanity that have passed away. Justice is so unlimited we can compass only a part of it, according to the knowledge we possess, and have cultivated the principal subject of the development. No people or nation can make laws

---

[1] This has reference to forget-me-not seeds which she sent me from Sweden.

to govern any other nation or people who can succeed them or figure on this planet. What can finite man do to control the Infinite? Can he gather and control the winds and the seasons as they come and go with all their powerful influences on the globe? No; neither can he gather and control the developments of minds, or subject them to any law that he may enact. History records the rise and fall of empires; behold, they have all passed away; each gives place to another form of government, better adapted to the wants and conditions of the then existing humanity. Dear friend, the heavenly trees are filled with divine fruit, whose beauty is reflected to earth. Truth is mightier than man, sharper than a two-edged sword, and it will mow down every obstacle in the way of progress. The spirit world is united in trying to lay the corner-stone of a temple so large that it will contain the whole human family. Oh, how grand when all can offer up the highest tribute of love to the divine unfolding spirit, and receive the sacred knowledge and love which shall bring humanity together in peace and harmony, then in truth all will be free. It gives me renewed strength to see the new and beautiful ideas floating about, spirit messengers wafted to earth, blending with man, woman and child as they go forth clearing the pathway to their eternal home, where all is love and harmony. The light of this beautiful truth is fast dawning, and suffering mortals will awake in joy to the light of it, and be crowned in the glory of the morning. It is not hard for spirits to communicate with friends on earth, but often difficult to have conditions. Man must have some spirituality in his soul before he can realize the truth that his loved ones are waiting, willing to help him upwards as they stand on the bright, celestial shore. Dear friend, I am sure I am gaining power, and would be able to say a great deal in a short time through this medium if no change of conditions come. I hope to help you to do what you so much desire. I can go to my dear friends across the water and help you by impressing them that all is true. Now I must withdraw, but will be very happy to come again to you, and give you all the knowledge I can. I am glad to see you so interested in learning what can only be taught by those who have passed the sands of earth life, and are happy exploring the unexplored field of life beyond. Good by, go on, fear not, the course you pursue is right. Your true friend in spirit life,

"Fredrika Ehrenborg."

On the 24th of May, from 9 to 12 A. M., the same highly esteemed spirit friend wrote on the slate:

"Good morning, my dear friend. I greet you this morning, united with so many of your loved ones. Your beautiful mother says it would not be heaven if we were shut out from the knowledge of our friends in the form. No, it could not be heaven if it made us selfish. I am glad you have reached that part of life and find bright rays daily. Freedom brings its own reward, and the light that has been given to you will enable you to have yours while life lasts. You will never be bereft of friends on this shore. You will have them in both spheres. Is it not grand to be able to understand, and even more, to appreciate, this knowledge? Light is pouring in, and the minds of men are becoming more active every day. Mankind are like hungry children who want food; yes, so great do they crave the knowledge of the immortality that it will take firm reasoning and true workers to supply them. We rejoice, for we are sure that progress is rapid. Earth friends often wonder what spirits find to do. If they could realize even half the wonderful work that is going on, they would be astonished that spirits had accomplished so much for the welfare of humanity. I am so happy my soul expands in love. I feel I am young, and I am, for I am born again. I am contented to have struggled so many years in earth life, for it has brought me grand reward. All trials are worth the privilege and pleasure we enjoy when we reach our spirit home. I can see now that it is no hiding-place in man's true nature, and if they are not learned upon the terrestrial planet, they will have to learn before they can become celestial angels. Selfishness is cold and freezing, love is genial and warms up the human soul, and thereby will promote its happiness. Let love be cultivated by man, for it is a favorite flower, the flower of life and the beauty of the soul, and by it humanity is renewed continually and brought to the newness of life's beauty, truth, beauty and higher spheres of eternal existence, and without it man can never understand or have any conception of his heavenly home. Oh, if love were the ruling influence, sorrow would be hard to find, heart aches would be nowhere felt. An early writer said: 'If you can not love him whom you have seen, how can you love them whom you have not seen and be beloved in return?' In loving one another we love God, for God is love. His love is manifesting in man. Oh, that it may be cultivated, and not destroyed. Dear friend, I feel I have given you an introduction at least in my three letters of what I believe would be a benefit to man if they could but understand how much depends upon them, not alone for themselves, but for the welfare and happiness of others. I will be able, as conditions are given, to write of my surroundings in my beautiful home, where all is love and harmony, peace reigns and all willing to submit to the ruling power. You have done more good than you are aware of. It is the greatest workers that always feel they are doing least. You send forth subjects that give new ideas to those who read them, awakening interest without any desire on their part. As I said before, if conditions are not interrupted, you will have much to read and to write. I have said all on this subject that I can, but I am not at a loss for something more to write about, for in spirit home how many beautiful things that have never yet been talked about too glorious to be enjoyed without giving the knowledge of their existence to our earth friends! A circle surrounds you this morning of loved ones near and dear, and your mother is cherished in loving kindness by children, children's children. Emil is a bright spirit, and will be able to give much knowledge to those who are a great deal older. Dear friend, I must withdraw and obey the law that governs my comings. All looks well for you so far as I see. No one can be really happy until their spirit is free to enjoy that happiness which is permanent, for all earthly pleasures are but temporary. Farewell for the present. In God's love may you continue your journey until you arrive on the mount where no dark ravines can intervene your happiness. Good bye for the present. Your sincere friend in spirit life,

"Fredrika Ehrenborg."

CHAPTER III.

REMARKABLE MATERIALIZATION SEANCE—LETTERS FROM MRS. EHRENBORG AND OTHERS DESCRIBING INHABITANTS OF PLANETS.

In the evening of the same day I was at a materializing seance at Mrs. Cooper's, where the following persons besides myself were present: Mr. Cooper, his wife, Mrs. Annie Cooper, the medium; Dr. Joseph R. Wittemore, No. 50 Dayton street; John Winterborn, No. 19 Freeman avenue; Mr. Oberline, Mr. S. G. Anderson, and Mr. Charles Wilhelm, all of Cincinnati.

First, Mrs. Cooper sat herself in full gas-light by the small covered stand, under which was placed three bells, a walking stick, and my small spring music-box, after I had wound it up. Soon after the spirits moved the box up and down and put it on end during playing, which we could see, because I put the box only half under the curtain. As soon as the playing stopped, the box was taken entirely under and finally pushed out for me to wind up. The bells were ringing and the walking stick was held up and extended to all of us to take hold of, which we did, and the spirits shook hands with us in that way. I had laid Madam Ehrenborg's photograph on the table, and I expressed a wish that she would materialize, when on the slate, which Mrs. Cooper held under the table-leaf, was written: "Good evening, friends; yes, I am with you; I will try to appear; we are so happy." The gas was now turned down, but not lower than we could see each other right well, and Mrs. Cooper took her seat in a chair behind the curtains stretched across a corner of the room, and soon after a lady spirit greeted Dr. Wittemore, who, he said, was his first wife. His sister also came and nodded to him. Then came a sister to Anderson and a sister to Mr. Winterborn, together with his mother, who took a flower from him, and nodded to him very cordially. A spirit lady did the same to Mr. Wilhelm. Mr. Cooper brought now my music instrument, orgamina, from the upper room and placed it before me and I played on it with the crank. Soon after a lady spirit came, dressed in a white shining robe, and beckoned to me, when Mrs. Cooper, who was not in a trance, invited me to come up to the curtain where the spirit stood in the opening, and I asked if it was my friend Madam Ehrenborg who died in Sweden, Europe, eight years ago, and she bowed and nodded assent. Mr. Winterborn gave me a flower, which I took and offered to Madam Ehrenborg, who took it, smelled it, and stuck it under my nose to smell, and afterwards kept it. I expressed my gladness to see her and she made graceful bows, which I answered with mine. I then went back to the music instrument to play, when Madam Ehrenborg came out again with a beautiful long piece of lace on her arm and wafted it to and fro, and afterwards dematerialized before us. After that came a lady and sat herself in the rocking-chair, and there dematerialized before us. Mrs. Cooper took now a standing position in the opening of the curtain, when a male spirit came out, stood beside her, and kissed her. When Mrs. Cooper took her seat behind the curtain again a tall gentleman spirit came dressed in some kind of a uniform, with a glittering star on his right breast, and Mr. Winterborn offered him a nosegay, which he took and held out with his hand, swinging his arm up and down, keeping time to the music of the orgamina and that for a long time. As he came out the next time he took hold of the rocking chair outside the curtain before him and swung it over his head for a long time, and afterwards lowered it down to about a foot from the floor, when he dropped it. At the same time we saw Mrs. Cooper, who expressed her anxiety lest the chair might fall on her. Next he placed himself at the opening of the curtain, when a lady spirit took her place at his left side, and they kissed each other. Mrs. Cooper asked for a glass of water, which Mr. Cooper went after, intending to give it to his wife, but the gentleman spirit took it from him and gave it to Mrs. Cooper, who drank the water out of the glass. The same spirit sat himself in the lap of Mrs. Cooper and kissed her after he had placed a flower in her hair. Mrs. Cooper was coughing, and Mr. Winterborn gave two cough lozenges to the spirit, who gave them to Mrs. Cooper. The uniformed gentleman spirit came again out and took the rocking-chair with his right hand and swung it very vigorously over his head for a good while, then put it down. All the other spirits had white robes shining as snow, and all of us were exceedingly gratified at such wonderful performance.

The 29th of June, 1881, among other valuable communications, came:

"Good morning, my dear friend; it is with the greatest pleasure I again come to communicate with you. Your star of hope is increasing in brightness. I called on you and your dear lady last night (your night). You appreciate the beauties of the heavens, it was indeed grand to the natural eye." (My wife and I last evening were on the roof of our house on Mount Auburn looking at the comet and the stars.) "Oh, I thought if I could lift the veil and show you the inner life so brightly beaming once again, what joy it would give. I have visited three planets, each one had a distinct race (of people) and different one from another, and had mostly white skin, walked erect, were all of the same physical shape, very much like the inhabitants of our planet; their features are more regular and not much contrast in size. On the first planet they were small in stature—about four feet high. On the second sphere, about five feet high and of uniform size and shape. On the third they were six feet high, with large limbs and muscles, language quite different from ours, but were highly educated; eat no animal food, subsist entirely on vegetable. The day and night are of equal length; and as this last named planet was most interesting to me I will speak first of it: They have a better system of astronomy than we do and understand it more perfectly. This planet has large water courses and a great deal of commerce. They have no religion, such as Christians call religion, but a very high order of morals. They know little of the immortality of the soul. They have no wars, no courts nor prison houses, and murder is unheard of. They have no kings, no politics, no religion, consequently no wars. They live in perfect harmony; women suffer very little inconvenience in bearing children; the families are large, with eight or ten children; they are contented and happy. They have better painters in coloring in both landscapes and portraits. Their architecture is perfection; their buildings are the most beautiful I ever beheld. The climate is genial the year round, never too hot, and never necessary to have fire to keep warm; but little variety in temperature. Dear friend, I could say much more if I had power. I thank you for your kind attention. I will be able another time. Good bye for the present. Your sincere friend in spirit life,

"Fredrika Ehrenborg."

The 27th of July at a seance at Mrs. Cooper's, her control informed me that we meet to-day under disturbed conditions, and when I asked Mrs. Cooper what that meant, she said her husband wanted her to move back to Louisville, as his prospects there now were better, and she had concluded to do so, in consequence of which she intended to pack up her furniture immediately after the present seance. Madam Ehrenborg wrote now a communication from which I will extract the following: "This dear, good woman, whom the angels will bless, is the first channel through which I have been able to reach earth and friends in this way, and now to be disturbed and taken away for a while is a loss to us. I could go to her, but not write as I write to you, the friendship formed between us before I passed away gives me strength and desires I might not have in any other way, but this form of condition will not last long. * * * I will try to communicate to you whenever condition is given, it is so easy for me to write here. There are but few who I could say so much through in so short a time. * * * Mrs. Cooper, if you will sit for me next Wednesday from there (Louisville) I hope to be able to write frequently, but not like if he was present. Good bye for the present. Your most sincere friend in spirit land.

"Fredrika Ehrenborg."

Mrs. Cooper promised to do as she was requested and we agreed, as the spirits wanted, that I at usual hour, 9 o'clock A. M., should sit alone at home the same time as the seance should take place in Louisville. Wednesday, the 3d of August, I picked a few flowers and kept some of them with me, as my spirit son Emil directed, and the rest were placed in a glass on the stand, which was covered, and under it I put Madam Ehrenborg's photograph and her letters sent me from Sweden. The 5th of August I received a letter from Miss Sadie Hare, No. 222 St. Catherine street, Louisville, Ky., wherein she states that "Mrs. Cooper came quite a distance to our home the 3d of August to fulfill her engagement with you and the dear spirit friends, not having conditions at her sister's that would enable her to give opportunities to the spirits. We live a long distance apart and some distance from the street railway, but you know the distance would have to be very great to prevent Mrs. Cooper from keeping a spiritual engagement. * * With this you will find your communications which I have copied. Respectfully yours,

"Sadie Hare."

"Louisville, *August 3, 1881.*

"Yes, we see the photographs of our dear friend, and he has obeyed the request made. We wish we could bring just one of the white blossoms he has gathered for the occasion to you. The dear spirit friends he desired to hear from were present when he made preparations for conditions to assist them to come to you. Tell him all will be well with him. The knowledge he has gained of the spirit world will not decay like the blossoms he has gathered in his beautiful bouquet. His friend Doc." The control of Mrs. Cooper.

"We have come, and see that you have had a long distance to come to make conditions for us. Emil is with me, and we will do all we can to write a message to my dear friend C. G. Helleberg. I have reached the medium through which I have been able to write so much in so short a time. I find her much troubled and disturbed and will not be able to say to you what I could if you were present as in former conditions, but remember what I have told you, my work in spirit life has only began, and I yet hope to say much to you and through this medium. All the changes that come to our friends in the form are not pleasant for them, but changes that come to us in our spirit home increases the happiness and joy that we dwell in, but not alone, for there is no real happiness that can be enjoyed alone, for we are united in love and harmony, and we are happy that the change called death does not sever the friendship formed in earth life. Progression is the highest ambition of all good spirits.

"Man does not see or know the need of knowledge while in earth life, but when he enters real life and knows there is no turning backwards he feels forced by law of goodness to help all those who are yet in darkness; but, my friend, there are so many who are forgotten as soon as the spirit has left the form and believed to be dead by all they once held dear. I feel like repeating over and over again the joy I continually receive, being remembered by you who have opened the avenue for me to give and receive. Be assured that your reward will come and inscribed in bright, shining letters on a banner of truth—your work well done, good and faithful servant. Emil is present, and desires to send a few words to his papa and mamma. I know, my dear friend, how you missed the interview this morning you would have enjoyed so much; but be reconciled, they are more disturbed than our dear medium; but could she behold the bright spirits that stand in circle around her she would not despair. It will not be long till the way is cleared and we can draw nearer to communicate through her to you, and of every thorn comes a blessing, the severest cross is a crown to those who are willing to bear for the sake of truth and progression. I desire, my dear friend, to have these interviews repeated. Had there not been a kind, genial lady to sit for you to copy what was written I would not have been able to say this much in a strange place. I thank you, my young friend, for assistance and willingness on your part, and remember, though the act may seem small to you, it is worth gratitude from us, and you may rely upon an increase of spiritual influence to assist you. Accept this, my dear friend; I hope to say more again. Your most sincere friend in spirit life,

"Fredrika Ehrenborg."

CHAPTER IV.

MADAM EHRENBORG AND OTHERS MATERIALIZE.

I received several other valuable letters of my spiritual friends from Louisville, and in one of them, the 18th of August, Madam Ehrenborg wrote:

"A request has been made for Mrs. Helleberg to write a letter to her sister Emma and her father, that it may enable them to remain long enough to communicate that she may hear direct from them, for they are often with her, and want her to know it is not wrong for them to come or for her to look for them."

In consequence of this I persuaded my wife to write a letter to them, which she did, and I sealed it up with red sealing wax, with my seal on, and sent it by mail to Mrs. Cooper, without any superscription. On the 25th of August we received a letter from Miss Hare and Mrs. Cooper, together with my wife's sealed letter unopened, and a long and beautiful letter from her spirit sister, Emma, who had also answered for her father, which was so true and striking that her fear melted away, and concluded to investigate these strange facts. In October, Mrs. Cooper revisited Cincinnati, during which time my wife and I had several very satisfactory seances, and on invitation from her we were present at a social materialization seance on the 28th of said month, in the evening, in company with the following persons: Mr. and Mrs. Stebbins, Miss Sadie Hare, Mrs. Gano, Mr. and Mrs. Green, Mr. Cooper's mother, Mr. and Mrs. Macky, Mr. and Mrs. Nicely, Miss Sneider, Mrs. Artzman, Dr. Taylor and Mr. Winterborn. A curtain was stretched across a corner of the room, and the small stand was put on the floor, and under it was placed two call bells, a big brass bell, and a drum, with sticks and a walking stick. When Mr. Stebbins played on the violin, or we sung or played on the orgamina, the spirits kept time with the bells and drum. The walking stick was pointed to different individuals of the company, who had mental questions answered when they took hold of the uplifted stick. Mr. Stebbins put the end of the bow under the table, and the fiddle he laid on the floor, about a foot from the table, when the spirits played on it. The table was also lifted up and down, keeping time with our music. When Mrs. Cooper took her seat behind the curtain soon after, several spirits materialized to many of their relatives and friends, who recognized them, among whom were Miss Mary Muth and Madam Ehrenborg. I and my wife went up to the curtain, when Miss Mary Muth touched my wife's hand and took a flower from her. Afterwards Madam Ehrenborg came in full form, dressed in a fine dark suit, with a black lace cap, and when my wife asked if it was Mrs. Ehrenborg, she nodded her head smilingly several times, and then dematerialized. We took our seats, but Madam Ehrenborg came again twice, when I went up to the curtain with Mr. Stebbins, who also saw her very plainly, how she nodded to me and kissed my hand, which was touched by her lips, and had a warm feeling. She afterwards dematerialized before us. At the same time this took place we saw and conversed with Mrs. Cooper, who is never in a trance state at any time. When we came home we examined Madam Ehrenborg's photograph, and we found her dress and every thing else apparently exactly the same as that in which the photograph was taken. Her features were also the same. I had seen her materialized several times before, but always in shining white robes, and now she took on the same garment as that worn when the photograph was taken, probably to convince my wife of her identity.

CHAPTER V.

INVESTIGATIONS BY MRS. JENNIE M'KEE—FIRST LETTER FROM EMANUEL SWEDENBORG, ETC.

After Mrs. Cooper moved to Louisville I made acquaintance with Mrs. Jennie McKee, a real lady of high moral and truthful qualities, who had wonderful medial gifts, and permitted me to come to her residence, No. 47½ Sherman avenue, Cincinnati, for a slate-writing seance weekly, every Thursday, from 9 to 11 A. M. The spirits wrote independent, in broad daylight, when she held the slate under the stand, which was never covered with any thing, and with a pencil so small (about one-eighth part of a common wheat grain) that no human fingers in the body could write with it. I commenced with her the 4th of August, 1881, and continued until she passed away to the higher life, the 17th of November the same year. During that time I received many highly valuable and remarkable communications and gifts, of which I will only mention a few. On the 8th day of September there appeared among other communications on the slate the following:

"My friend, I come from a higher sphere of light and truth, in compliance with your request, and I greet you this morning in God's most holy name. I will speak to you not as I would have done when inhabited in earth form, but with a more expanded vision, and the more profound knowledge and the clearer understanding of the fundamental laws and governing principles of the Great Ruler of the universe. In those days in which I wrote it would have been a very unwise and dangerous thing to have given these spiritual manifestations to the people, from the fact that they were not prepared to receive the blessings, and the ultimate desire for the amelioration of mankind would have been defeated, and the result would have been disastrous."

I had wished a clearer understanding about our guardian spirits, and on the slate came:

"At the time of birth there are two self-constituted guardians, one from the light sphere and one from the dark, and as the child advances toward maturity, the number is greatly increased; but whether good or bad, depends entirely upon the persons themselves. Thus, for instance, if man leads a life of depravity and vice, he naturally attracts spirits of a like character; on the other hand, if a man leads a moral life of purity, bearing in his heart love and good will to others, he is surrounded by pure spirits, who are attracted by those elements. Thus, my friend, you see how essential it is, both for happiness here and through all eternity, that you conduct yourself so that the pure spirit of love can come and minister to you. I must leave, but will shortly come again."

Here I said to Mrs. McKee: "If he signs his name, I would like to have the slate, so I could show it to my wife;" and he said to her (but I could not hear him): "Put a paper on the slate." I cut a leaf from my annotation pocket book, and we put it on the slate loose, and Mrs. McKee held the slate, with the paper and a short lead pencil on it, under the table, and on the paper, now in my possession, was the following:

"Dear heart, so true to my memory, my blessing with you,

"Emanuel Swedenborg."

On the 13th of October, at a seance by Mrs. McKee, from 9 to 9:30 A. M., the following communication appeared on the slate:

"My beloved, I am with you, and I greet you with my blessing in the name of the Most High and Ruling Power, and not only is it I who bless you, you have attracted to you a number of highly exalted spirits, who love you for your singleness of purpose and purity of heart, with which you are promulgating the teachings you receive from us; that is why you have been selected by us, because you have been upright and moral in your life; because those who wish to investigate would be more impressed than did the communication come from other sources. Fear not, we will be with you, and each word will have weight. You must expect to be criticised and doubted; but again I say, fear not, we are with you, and will turn the thought of the people. We shall eventually see our efforts crowned with success. We appeal to the senses; it would be a vain and useless thing to set up a higher authority than man's own conscience, for that is the last final tribunal at which he is judged. The errand of life, the education, unfolding and strengthening the combination of the mind, the exigencies of business, the duties of citizenship, the cares of the household, all this requires the utmost seriousness of purpose and activity; but activity is neither in the development of manhood. It is far more essential that the mind and moral nature should have careful cultivation. Man should not care so much concerning the short period of natural life. From this side, through us who live by deeds, not years, in thought and feeling, instead of figures on the dial, by the happiness we produce, is our only gauge of time. There is an embodiment of selfishness underlying the human family which will first have to be eradicated through education, and it is the desire of the spirit world that man should be a brother to his fellow-man. I go now, but will be with you as often as I can. I leave my blessing for you and your household.

"Swedenborg."

"My friend, I come to say how much I enjoy and sympathize with you, that those who were blind are beginning to see, and are in better condition for the reception and appreciation of the spiritual blessing which is being prepared for you and yours by the loved ones who are gone before. I have brought my dear life companion with me this morning, who is working with me in acquiring the knowledge which will be necessary for you in the fulfillment of the mission you have been selected for to give out the knowledge of this glorious philosophy. It is the truth, for it is vouched for by the testimony of every atom, every bright world you observe in the firmament, and lastly by the spirit of the past man made perfect. You may be called fanatic, but if spiritualism is fanaticism, it is of more value to mankind than the whole circle of the sciences. We are called away now, but will come this evening.

"Fredrika."

"Dear papa, there is much joy and rejoicing among your spirit band. I am so happy that I can come to dear mamma, and have her receive me as you do. Kiss her for me. The power is too far gone to write any more.

"Emil."

On the 20th of October, 1881, between 9 and 11 A. M., at a seance with Mrs. McKee, the following communication appeared on the slate:

"Good morning, my friend. I am here, and greet you with my love and my blessing as the one chosen by me to help me in correcting the teachings I have put forth, and which at that time were not clearly understood even by myself, consequently I failed to render myself sufficiently intelligible to be properly understood by others. Now these mistakes must be rectified, and the erroneous impression replaced by the truth. I am preparing my statements, and they will be given to you in proper time through the channels we have chosen. I have chosen you as my assistant, well knowing your loyalty, steadfastness of purpose and your fearless disposition, so like what my own was, so it would be a matter of perfect indifference whether you received commendation of the people or only arouse their condemnation. It was this prominent characteristic which proved the attractive power that has drawn me to you. I ask no one to give up his principles; I simply desire to place truth before him, and let each individual reason according to the light surrounding him. Surely truth can defend itself, so we will let it speak for itself. I am happy and content with my surroundings, but I come to bring to the children of my love, the people of the new church, more light, if they will only receive it. I am impressed more fully each time I revisit your earth sphere that, had I lived at the present day, my labors would have been understood and appreciated, and I should not have felt that my best efforts were but a sad failure in comparison to what I expected or desired. I am now called away, so I now leave for this time, but will be with you soon. Good bye. God bless you and yours.

"Swedenborg."

On the 27th of October, 1881, at Mrs. McKee's, Swedenborg gave me a short communication, both on slate and paper, and afterwards came:

"Good morning, my friend, Swedenborg has been called away, but he has brought me to say a word and to assist in promulgating the truth. Many high and elevated spirits are banding together to spread the truth.

"Polheim."[2]

On the 3d of November, 1881, I had a seance with Mrs. McKee, and after the slate had been under the bare stand for about ten minutes a tap was heard, by which sign it was taken out from

---

[2] This Polheim was Sweden's greatest architect, mathematician and builder, who projected the canal between Stockholm and Gottenburg.

under the stand, and five exceedingly beautiful, fresh flowers, giving out a delicious perfume, were on the slate, and little dew drops had made some wet spots under them. On the slate was written the following:

"Good morning, my friend. I bring you some flowers. Let them convey to you the dearest essence of the high power to produce. They are the handiwork of God. In them we see His ever living presence.

"Fredrika Ehrenborg."

Afterwards the following communication appeared:

"Good morning, my beloved. I am again with you, weighty with rich blessings for you and yours, and I come also with a heart overflowing with love, tenderness and gratitude, that I am permitted, through the goodness and wisdom of the most High Power, to return, and through you, my trustworthy assistant, give my thoughts and ideas to the people. We love our mediums, our channels and our doorway, through which we come to love and bless. Take no heed of any unkind remarks, it is only an evidence of ignorance. Keep straight on, turn neither to the right nor to the left, continue to scatter seeds by the way-sides, which will furnish food for thought, and thought will lead to investigation. Investigation must necessarily lead in the acknowledgment of the truth. You can not expect to convince at once—it must be the work of time—and bear in mind, no one ever yet sought to benefit mankind who was not placed under the dark ban of suspicion. As you say, nothing can be gained by denunciation. Keep on. My blessing with you.

"Swedenborg."

CHAPTER VI.

MRS. M'KEE PASSES AWAY AND HER SPIRIT ARRANGES HER OWN FUNERAL.

When the seance was over, I at once took the flowers to Mrs. Minor's to have them arranged according to her art for preservation and now have them in all their original beauty. The 17th of November, 1881, I went to Mrs. McKee for a slate-writing seance, as for some time I have been used to do every Thursday morning at 9 o'clock, where I met at the door her step-father, R. J. William, who informed me that his daughter Jennie had, half an hour before, passed away to the spiritual world, and invited me up on the floor above to see her body. In the death-room I found my friend, the wonderful clairvoyant and trance medium, Mrs. Anna Rall, and Jennie's mother, who found that her head was not quite cold. From the house of mourning I went to Mrs. Minor's for the five flowers I had received from my dear spirit friend, Mrs. Fredrika Ehrenborg, through the medial power of Mrs. McKee, the 3d of November, and which now were preserved under glass, and afterwards went to have a seance at Mrs. Green's, where I placed those beautiful flowers on the small stand between us. Soon we heard writing on the slate and a tap, when we found on it the following communication:

"Good morning, dear papa. How sad for you to look upon the face this morning, not yet cold, that had afforded you so much real happiness, and pure as the flowers before you that came through her medial powers. She entered the spirit world to meet the loved ones gone before. Her suffering is no more. She saw you, and I shook hands with her. She knew me, and she was all smiles. She was glad she passed away on the morning she had an engagement with you; so your heavenly influences were there to aid her spirit. She hoped for it. She will be able to communicate to you soon and tell you how she found the new life. She will write immediately, she understands it. Dear papa, try to make a house not of mourning; she wants joy, she is free from suffering and able to communicate. Will see her own funeral and wishes to have a real spiritualist's funeral, becoming one who has passed away in its full faith. She wants Mrs. Green to repeat that beautiful poem that she so much admired: 'I *Still* Live' (herself). *I would like Mr. Green, with others, to make some consoling remarks. The song 'There is no death,' sung.* She says that every thing so far has turned out all right, and she wants every thing done according to her desire. They all know what a devotee she was in spiritualism." (Here I mentioned to Mrs. Green that I would go back to the house of mourning and tell them of this as soon as possible, and now came.) "That is just it. She told me all and requested me to write it. She wants them to cast away the thoughts of her old body from their minds, and to think her free spirit moving through the house as of old. She wants her dear old parents not to mourn. She wants all the mediums next to her immediate family, and spiritualists, to strengthen her so she can manifest, if possible. She says these are her wishes; they can do as they please. Dear papa, I have done my duty this morning for her beautiful free spirit, and happy for the honor conferred upon me as her amanuensis. We have nothing more to communicate this morning, only she wants Mrs. Rall, her near and dear friend, to control affairs as far as she can, as she knows her wishes and desires, and knows she will please her and do what is right. Love to dear mamma; kiss her for me.

"Emil."

"Mrs. McKee says many thanks for your kindness She will be with you often. Much love to all.

"Emil."

We were present at her beautiful funeral, where Jennie herself spoke through Mrs. Rall over her own body, and it was in truth remarked from the people that this was the most soul-uplifting funeral services they ever had witnessed. The spirit communicates with me often.

CHAPTER VII.

INVESTIGATIONS WITH MRS. GREEN—
REMARKABLE DARK TRUMPET SEANCE AT WHICH I
RECEIVED A MOST BEAUTIFUL FLOWER FROM MY
SON EMIL AND MISS MARY MUTH.

"My investigations through the excellent medium, Mrs. Green, commenced the 2d of September, 1881, and I received many interesting communications from my dear and near relatives, which I value very highly, but naturally would not have the same value for the general reader, and therefore I deem it best to exclude most of them and take in only writings from exalted spirits who are more generally known.

The 19th of September came:

"From the higher sphere of light I come
To teach you the beauties of our home,
And to impart to you the golden truth
And make you feel its real worth.

"And to my dear old friend, your wife,
I wish to prove a future life,
And to assist her while she remains here,
And help to guide her to our heavenly sphere.

"Oh, the beautiful birds that sing their lay,
Come to bless me every day,
The flowers of fragrance, sweet and rare,
And heavenly music fills the air.

"From your friend,
"Fredrika Ehrenborg."

The 20th of October, 1881, I was present at Mrs. Green's trumpet seance in the evening in company with the following persons: Mr. Green, the medium's husband; Mr. and Mrs. Stebbins, a reporter from the "Enquirer," who gave his name as Johnson, and Mr. Walker. On the stand was placed three slates, one of which was my own, three trumpets, one glass of water, and my spring music-box. On the floor stood the big tin trumpet and by it laid my guitar, and not far from Mr. Stebbins was his fiddle. After the light was put out and the doors locked I wound up my music-box and put it on the right hand corner of the stand before me. Soon after it was taken away while playing and carried around all over our heads, and some of us were touched with it. Finally it came back to me and was placed in my left hand with the spirit, whose hand I touched with both my hands. I wound it up again and the spirit took it away and carried it around the same as before, but when it came back it was placed on the left hand corner of the stand, and I laid the key close by it. Afterwards I played my orgamina when the spirit voices of both sexes joined in with their songs, and so they did when we sang.

I intended to wind up the music-box again and felt for it on the corner, when I discovered that both the box and key were gone. Soon after we heard the box playing and going over our heads as before, and the box was replaced on the corner of the stand with the key on top. All the trumpets and the guitar were moving around in the air high above our heads, the guitar was played on in time with the music, and we all were touched and stroked on different parts of our bodies with these implements. The guitar was laid in my lap, and I sang a Swedish song, accompanied by the guitar, when we heard a spirit voice singing with me, and I and the others heard the words pronounced by the spirit, which I declare were the same Swedish words which I sung. Mrs. Stebbens was clasped around her neck by her spirit daughter Ida, who whispered to and patted both her and Mr. Stebbins. Mrs. Green and Mrs. Stebbens saw several spirit lights, and Mr. Walker was informed by striking and tolling on the big tin trumpet that his father in Kansas would soon pass away. I felt for my music-box again, intending to wind it up, when I, to my great surprise, found a fresh, beautiful flower on top of it, and my slate was placed in my hand. Soon after the seance was closed and when the room was lighted up, we found written on one slate the name of the reporter, and on my slate the following:

"Dear papa, we present you the flower we promised you some time ago. The passion flower.

"Emil and Mary."

It was a large, very beautiful, quite fresh flower, which I now have preserved in a glass jar with deodorized alcohol. On seeing this flower my wife's idea was that the flower had been brought from some garden, and I thought the spirits made it, which caused me, at a slate-writing seance the 24th of October, to ask which of us was right. On the slate was this answer:

"Mary and I, with the assistance of the medium's band, *created it* for you and dear mamma, and you will find a dove in the center."

On a close examination we found to our astonishment a small dove there.

CHAPTER VIII.

SURE IDENTITY OF MY FATHER-IN-LAW—MADAM EHRENBORG WRITES TO ME IN SWEDISH.

On the 8th of December, 1881, I and my wife had a slate-writing seance in the forenoon, and were present in the evening at a trumpet seance with Mrs. Green, and as my wife received a strong convincing test through the name of her father, it is necessary before relating the facts to make a short sketch of a part of his life. He was a Swedish nobleman, named Otto Jacob Natt och Dag, who, by the favor of the dethroned King Gustaf Adolf the Fourth, was educated in the military academy, and afterwards served as officer in a rank regiment in Stockholm, which the new King Charles the Fourteenth, Johan, the former Napoleon's General Bernadott, looked upon with great favor. This young nobleman wrote an anonymous book about reorganizing the Swedish army, in which many good and necessary reforms were proposed. This book was not intended for sale, but a few copies had been printed for his intimate friends. Some of his so-called friends reported this, and mentioned his name to the King, who became enraged that a young officer should dare to have the impertinence to interfere with his business, and want to teach him, who had such a vast experience in military affairs, the consequence of which was that he was transported to serve in a common infantry regiment, far up in the northern part of the country, a long distance from his near and dear relatives. Such treatment naturally made him feel bad, and he asked permission to travel in foreign countries, which he got, and went straight to Baden, in Germany, where he called on his former King, Gustaf Adolf, and was kindly received. There he republished his book in the German language, with some additions, which the Swedish minister reported to the King, who then considered him a traitor, and ordered his arrest, but his Swedish friends informed him of this in time, and he went to America under the name of Frederick Franks, which was the name of a German student, who gave him his passport, and which he afterwards adopted and used until his death. The King, Charles the Fourteenth, had him adjudged, unheard and absent, by a court for high treason, for daring to pay a visit to the dethroned King, and the judgment was that he should lose his place and rank in the army. Many years afterwards the King regretted his harsh and unjust treatment of his faithful, patriotic and skillful officer, and pardoned him, and ordered his Swedish minister at Washington to inform him of it, so he could go back and enjoy all his privileges; but his former guard officer had now been for many years a republican citizen, who, with his artistic and many other talents and business capacity, had made himself independent, and he never went back. Nobody here but the family knew any thing of his Swedish name, and my wife said to me that she would be more fully convinced of her father's identity if he would sign himself with that name.

In the slate-writing seance in the forenoon I had put my own slate, which Mrs. Green never touched, under the side of the stand nearest me, and on Mrs. Green's slate the following appeared:

"Put out the slate and see if any thing is on it?"

I did so, and on my slate the following sentence appeared:

"God bless you both is the wish of your exalted friend,

"Fredrika Ehrenborg."

Among other things was the following:

"Now, dear papa and mamma, we have done all we can this morning. Much love to you both. Grandpa will be with you to-night; Grandpa Helleberg, Mary and Julia, too, Emil, Gustaf and Charley. You will have many bright and beautiful spirits with you this evening to cheer you on your road to the beautiful spirit world. There all are in peace and happiness—Emil, Frances, Emma, Mary, Julia.

"Emanuel Swedenborg."

On the evening of the 8th of December, at the above-mentioned trumpet seance were present, besides me and my wife, the following persons: Mr. and Mrs. Stebbins, Mr. and Mrs. Taylor, Mrs. Catherine Remlin, Mr. and Mrs. Green and Mrs. Boggs. We had spirit singing and talking, with many other remarkable manifestations. Among the spirits who spoke were Garfield, Washington and Lincoln, three ex-Presidents. Two slates were put on the table by Mr. Green before the light was put out, and I had that afternoon bought two very small silica slates, of which I gave one to my wife, who held it in her hand, and the other, in the dark, I put on the corner of the table nearest me, which nobody else knew any thing about. When the seance was over several names and messages were written on the two big slates, and on mine was the following on both sides:

"My Dear Daughter—Oh, how happy I am that I have found a way to communicate to you. I will be with you often.

"O. J. N. D."

On the other side appeared:

"My Dear Daughter—According to promise I am with you. I have many things to tell you. With my heart full of love for you,

"O. J. N. D."

These were the initials of my wife's father's Swedish name, Otto Jacob Natt och Dag, and we were highly pleased with the result. Subsequently he communicated often, signing his name in full, as above.

On the 23d of March, 1882, at Mrs. Green's, among other communications, was the following:

"Dear Papa—All of your Swedish friends are here, and intend to use their influence to-day and give you a surprise before the seance is over. All are present except Swedenborg, who we expect very soon. We are not sure of success, but we intend to try. The surprise will be Grandpa Franks trying to communicate inside of the double slate, with your assistance holding the slate and all of your friends influence combined. Madam Ehrenborg withheld her message to-day to add her strength and help grandpa with his surprise to mamma and you. * * * Swedenborg has come; get the slate. This is all you will get from me to-day. Your loving son,

"Emil."

We cleaned the double slate and put it under the table, where I held on to one end of it and pressed the two slates together with my hand, while Mrs. Green held the other end, and we both felt and heard the writing going on inside the two slates. The writing continued about ten minutes, after which a tap was heard, when I took the slate out, opened it, and in my father-in-law's handwriting found the following communication, which I had photographed and electrotyped as seen opposite:

On the 23d of July, from 9 to 11 A. M., at Mrs. Green's, I had cheerful writings from our three sons and grand-daughter, Julia Muth first, and afterwards there appeared on the slate the following communication in the Swedish language:

"Dyra goda wän C. J. Helleberg! Jag prsenterar dig min Högaktning och evinnerlig wänskap.

"Fredrika Ehrenborg."

Which, translated into English is:

"Dear, good friend C. J. Helleberg, I present you my esteem and eternal friendship.

"Fredrika Ehrenborg."

I had it photographed, as shown.

> Dyra goda wän H. G. Helleberg,
> Jag presenterar dig min Högaktning
> och evinnerlig wänskap.
>
> Fredr: Ehrenborg
> 25 of July 1892
> medium Mrs Lizzi S. Green

CHAPTER IX.

INFORMATION OF A SPIRITUAL MARRIAGE—THE WEDDING AND THE WEDDING TOUR TO THE PLANET MARS.

For a long time I had regular slate-writing seances in the light and one dark trumpet seance every week at Mrs. Green's residence, No. 309 Longworth street, and at that time were generally present the following persons: Mr. and Mrs. Stebbins, Mr. and Mrs. Taylor, Mrs. Remlin, Mr. and Mrs. Helleberg, all of Cincinnati, and Mrs. Bogg, from Newport, Ky. In these trumpet seances the spirits not only played on musical instruments, which they carried over our heads, and very often touched us with them and their hands, but talked and sung to us with or without the trumpet. The 12th of January, 1882, our son Emil astonished us with the information that he was going to marry Miss Ida, the spirit daughter of Mr. and Mrs. Stebbins, and that she would be his spirit wife. In a slate-writing seance, the 16th of January, he informed me that Mr. Swedenborg would perform the nuptial ceremony, and who also had determined the wedding to take place on Washington's birthday—the 22d of February. We were also informed that the spirit, Mr. Henry Nieman, Ida's cousin, would be the groomsman, and the spiritual Miss Mary Muth her bridesmaid, and that a bridal trip had been arranged in which many bright and exalted spirits would take part, including Madam Ehrenborg. Mr. Swedenborg would make the wedding speech on the spiritual side, and he requested Mr. Green to make one on this side. Mr. and Mrs. Stebbins, my wife and I, agreed that this remarkable wedding ceremony should take place at Mr. Stebbins' residence at the appointed time—the 22d of February—and we concluded to ask the spirits who we should invite, and the 16th day of February, 1882, came on the slate the following names:

"Pa and ma Stebbins, papa and mamma Helleberg, Mr. and Mrs. Green and daughter, Mrs. Emma Muth, Mrs. Remlin, Mr. and Mrs. Taylor, Miss Nettie Williams, and Mrs. Keenan.

"Emil and Ida."

At a slate-writing seance, the 20th of February, came on the slate, among many other communications, the following:

"The ceremonies are to begin at four, and immediately after congratulation, supper. It will take one hour, Mr. Swedenborg says, to show the medium the ceremony and Mr. Green's address. When the vision is through, then Mr. Green, then supper, and, after that is settled, a trumpet seance.

"Emil."

According to this arrangement the above persons were all invited and present, except Mrs. Keenan and Miss Nettie Williams, who could not come, at the afternoon and evening seances the 22d, the 150th anniversary of Washington's birthday. In the afternoon we assembled at 3 o'clock P. M., and at 4 Mrs. Green was in full trance, and Swedenborg controlled her and blessed the contracting parties, after which Mr. Green made a very appropriate and beautiful address. A private clairvoyant fell in a trance and described not only the clothing of the bride and bridegroom, but many other spirits present. The bride's dress was pure, sparkling white, frosted with gold dust, with long train full of the finest lace, and a very beautiful veil, frosted also, and adorned with a handsome wreath on her head of white flowers set with three beautiful diamonds on her forehead. She had also a diamond brooch and necklace, with a splendid ring on her finger, and slippers on her feet to match. Our son Emil had knee-breeches of royal purple, with a beautiful white toga frosted with gold, and gold tassels and a purple and gold crown set with diamonds. (At a subsequent seance Emil said: "Mine was Mr. Swedenborg's selection, Ida's was Madam Ehrenborg's.") During the trance state of Mrs. Green, the spirit Winnie described the dresses in the same way as the private medium already had told us. After we had had a splendid repast the requested trumpet seance was arranged, at which all were present, and had the pleasure of being spoken to by Swedenborg, Emil, Ida, and many other spirits, and some of them patted us with their hands. Madam Ehrenborg and my wife's father, Otto Jacob Natt-och-Dag (Frederick Franks), sung Swedish with me, and Mrs. Jennie McKee took my hand and lifted my arm up and putting it over the table so I had to rise. It was a beautiful and most satisfactory and wonderful manifestation over which we all were highly delighted.

The 23d of February, 1882, came from our spirit friends the following:

"Good morning, dear papa, we are here yet, but will immediately after this sitting start on our bridal tour, accompanied by Swedenborg and a great many exalted spirits. We expect to return by next Thursday, then Mr. Swedenborg will give the marriage ceremonies, and we hope to have something nice to write you then. Mr. Swedenborg is very much pleased because he is able to speak and control Mrs. Green, and was very much pleased also with the way it was conducted on your side. He says altogether it was a splendid affair on both sides, and I think so too, and now I will let my wife, Mrs. Ida Helleberg, write. Your loving son,

"Emil Helleberg."

"Good morning, dear papa Helleberg; Emil makes me blush when he says my wife. It used to be a joke, but now it is a reality, and that is quite different. When we all meet on the evergreen shores of the summerland, then we will return the compliment and have the infair at our own home, no matter how far off it may be, you shall always receive our hospitality and our love in the cottage. With my heart full of love for you and dear mamma Helleberg and sister Emma, and my dear pa and ma, and Mrs. Green's family, I bid you good morning.

"Ida Stebbins Helleberg."

"Good morning, Mr. Helleberg: I was very much delighted with the exercises of yesterday afternoon and evening. It could not have been more perfect on both sides. I was with you all the time. It was witnessed by thousands of spirits with much interest and delight. Whatever Mr. Swedenborg, does in the spirit world causes great commotion and interest. He is in the spirit world like some of your great men here, a leader. His every word, look, and gesture, is chronicled by the spirits; therefore you may imagine the interest they manifest towards him. Nettie could not and would not leave mother. She is so lonely without me, but she was here heart and soul in spirit. With my highest regards for you all, I am your friend,

"Jennie."

"Good morning, my dear friend: As the marriage of our granddaughter to your son has united my son Edwin and your family, and that event caused or rather brought us in a positive condition, and enabled us to pick up the trumpet and manifest our appreciation of that event, I thought I would write a few lines in regard to this happy marriage, and to show our very high appreciation of this medium's family, for, as Ida said, it has brought sunshine to her dear pa and ma that they could not find any-where else outside the spirit communion, and express our very high appreciation of your son Emil, and that we feel very proud of them both, and of our hearts full of love for Edwin and his wife, and highest regards for yourself and family and Mrs. Green's family, we subscribe ourselves your dear spirit friends,

"Amariah Stebbins and Permelia Stebbins."

"Good morning, my friends, Mr. Helleberg and Mrs. Green: To say I was very much delighted, or, in fact, I have not language at my command to express to you my appreciation of yesterday's proceedings, and happy of the opportunity presented that I can write to-day. Winnie described me as I was. Love to my dear daughter and her husband (Edwin Stebbins), and regard to all,

"Thomas Kelly."

"Good morning, dear son: Father, brother, and all of us are here to give you our congratulations and to tell you how much we love dear Ida, and that she is so sweet and beautiful. We were all with you last night, and caressed you with the trumpet. It made us so happy. Father can not write to-day, but will soon. With our blessings on you and all, your loving mother,

"Ulrica Helleberg."

"Good morning: I must not fail to give a few words in appreciation of the marriage feast. It was splendid, and I was very much pleased with the ceremony spiritually and mortal. Love to dear Anna and yourself and highest regard to all. Francis, Emily, Susan and Joseph join me and send much love to all. With my prayers for you all, I bid you good bye.

"Fredrick Franks."

"Now, dear papa, we are all through, and Gustaf and Charles join in congratulations, and asked me to write for them, and tell you that they are so much pleased with their sister-in-law. Mary, Henry, and little Julia and Clarence, and many that I have not time to mention, join us with much love for all. Two souls with but a single thought, two hearts that beat as one, we bid you good bye,

"Emil and Ida."

The 2d of March came: "Good morning, my dear friend. The tourists, according to promise, have not returned. I have been sent as a messenger from Mr. Swedenborg to report to you that their reception on the planet Mars was so grand, and they are there so nicely entertained by the spirits of that planet that they have all been invited to participate in a similar feast to take place to-day, and they all send their love and best wishes to you, and hope to be with you at your next sitting. With my highest regard and well wishes for your future prosperity, I am your spirit friend,

"Polheim."

The 6th of March the exalted Swedenborg wrote on the slate: "Good morning, friends: I am here to give you the marriage ceremony I promised in pantomime on the 22d ultimo. It is brief, and does not include the address and prayer given on that occasion. * * * As you have already been united in the conjugal sense by the operation of the laws of spiritual attraction and magnetic affiliation, no formal cementation or consecration is needed, but in obedience to an ancient custom, originating in spirit life in the early dawns of the physical earth-planet, and from thence projected to mortal life, I have the pleasure of pronouncing the ceremony that blends you, in obedience to the custom stated, into blissful spiritual consociation as man and wife, which I now do in presence of the invited guests here assembled. In blissful happiness you are to live in peaceful joy, to move in heavenly love to act, so shall your onward march be unobstructed, and as you advance increasing in wisdom, expanding and abounding in love, and augmenting in power until the highest angels and seraphims shall claim you for angelic companionship. Now, while the choristers join in the marriage anthem, I present for your congratulations this spiritually mated couple, who I now introduce as Emil Gabriel Helleberg and Ida Stebbins Helleberg.

"Emanuel Swedenborg."

Just as Madam Ehrenborg's communications were being copied for the printer, the "Banner of Light"—the oldest spiritual paper in existence—of date July 1, 1882, was placed in my hands, in which I find a communication from Helen Barnard Densmore, of Philadelphia, in which she says:

"Philadelphia has been favored recently with a course of lectures from Mr. W. J. Colville, which have been well attended and received with appreciation. This truly inspired speaker is doing a great work in spreading the new gospel of spiritualism wherever he is called. His discourses are of a high order, in an intellectual and literary sense, as well as of great spiritual elevation. At one of the social receptions given to him at the residence of Colonel S. P. Kase, he gave a very interesting discourse on the physical life and development of the planets of our solar system as compared with the earth, which was listened to with an earnest attention and evident acceptance by those present. It was taught in this discourse that worlds were brought into existence for the sole purpose of furnishing a theater for souls to express themselves in matter upon, to the end of gaining knowledge and overcoming temptations in all forms and of all kinds; that these lives make up a system of embodiments which closes with the soul's triumph over all the evils to be found in material life.

"We were told that in Mercury the attainment of a high degree of physical perfection was the highest ambition of its inhabitants; that that planet was in a lower state of animal, vegetable and spiritual progress than the earth, and the cultivation of the soil was their almost universal occupation; that Venus was in a high state of artistic and æsthetic cultivation; that art and music were the dominant passions there, with less intellectual and spiritual development, sensuous delights every-where abounding, and the cultivation of the beautiful the highest aim of life. On the earth the demon to be overcome was declared to be intellectualism, man's intellect being here worshiped and deified at the expense of the spiritual.

"On Mars and Jupiter is to be found a much higher state of existence, matter being dominated by the spirit to a much greater degree than on either this earth or those planets nearest the sun; that exalted spirits from those planets, especially from Mars, are sent as especial embodiments to the earth, as teachers and messengers for spiritual truth.

"Life on the more distant planets from the sun, beyond Jupiter, was declared to be of such an exalted character that there is no language understandable on earth in which to depict its glories and achievements."

CHAPTER X.

DESCRIPTION OF THE JOURNEY TO MARS, AND WONDERFUL INFORMATION FURNISHED BY MADAM EHRENBORG.

"March 9, 1882. Our party of tourists, after having been carefully selected in accordance with their ability to utilize the magnetic currents that connect the planets in our solar system, and their adaptability to the electric and magnetic condition of Mars, whither we were bound, started on the journey at, according to your time, midnight, February 23. We proceeded without any incident of note until we reached Maluka Plains, where we met a party of excursionists on a visit to our planet earth. Maluka Plains, named after a great prophet of Mars, are located many millions of miles from the circling magnetic belts of earth, and immediately adjacent to the outer circle of the electro-magnetic atmosphere of Mars. We were surprised to find that these excursionists were acquainted with our guide and leader, Mr. Swedenborg, for he had frequently visited the most interesting points of our stellar system. He had even been at Mars in spirit while he was in the body of flesh, but he finds many things quite different from what he thought he had discovered during his spiritual visits when embodied. The party we met were on a tour of scientific exploration, and gladly availed themselves of information imparted by Swedenborg and Polheim, and we in return were greatly aided by data and information furnished by them to us. While this conference, or rather exchange of information, was in progress a courier was dispatched by our newly-made acquaintances to the spiritual magnates of Mars concerning our coming. I shall here stop and defer a description of our first reception until our next sitting.

"March 13. As we entered within the magnetic radius of Mars, and were emerging from the outer into the inner concentric circles, so characteristic of that planet, we met a reception committee of several thousand, and after formal greetings, we were escorted to a magnificent edifice, where were in waiting innumerable throngs of spiritual dignitaries and others to receive us. I here desire to remark that in my use of words I resort to your own vocabulary, for the thought language of the Marsians is quite different from the sound of your words, and to employ their terms would only confound you and militate against your proper conception and understanding of the narrative. For instance, I use the word edifice to indicate a structure, but they use an entirely different term and form of expression, and so on *ad infinitum*. The edifice referred to I am unable to describe, and it can only be fully understood in thought. In dimensions so great that your city of Cincinnati could be settled in one corner of it without attracting but very little attention. The material of which it is composed has no fitting representative on earth in its present state of development. Your diamonds and precious stones are as dim and unreflecting in comparison as a cloudy, murky day of autumn is to a bright summer day with the sun at meridian and the horizon unobstructed by cloud or a single mist. This comparison may serve to give you some idea of the absorbingly intense brilliancy of the mammoth structure, yet this is of itself but as a mote in the sunbeam to what I am assured exists in the immeasurable immensity of the higher creations in the inconceivable and boundless universe of God. Oh, how diminutive is this little ball of matter called earth, when we only measurably take in the vast immensity of the infinite domain of God. And poor, puny man, what a mere speck—a mere infinitisimal animalcule. As we approached this mammoth structure, it seemed to be tremulous with motion, and the motion, superinduced by such intensely penetrating, soul dazzling strains of music as to perfectly appal with ecstatic emotion our enraptured tourists. But for the preparation of us for it by the scientific spirits, who they called the Ulaetta, we could not have withstood it. I will give you this process of preparation on some future occasion, and I am sure it will be interesting to you and valuable when you come over. The ceremonies of reception were performed, not in speech, but in musical opera, which, singular to state, we were enabled to understand by the preparation mentioned. When I say musical opera I do not mean singing accompanied by music, but that the music itself was intensely operatic, and infused thought by the most astonishing and utterly inexplicable process into our interior soul consciousness. It was something worth years of suffering and pain to enjoy, and in contemplating its inconceivable grandeur I return to my own sphere, feeling how little I am, and to weep for the children of earth, still in ignorance and superstition, and I lift my voice in prayerful supplication to God to rend the veil, that poor humanity may obtain even faint glimpses of the gorgeous splendors of God's great kingdom; but I seem to hear a voice answering, Not yet; wait and be patient.

"March 20. We observed the most singular fact connected with the edifice wherein we were received. In approaching it we were unable to penetrate into its interior with our vision. It seemed to be a solid mass of exquisitely fine material, but on gaining admission into its interior, by some peculiar power that seemed to affect our spiritual vision and perceptions, we were enabled to see through and beyond it, and to perceive objects in the far distance. In other words, the whole structure seemed to vanish so far as to permit no obstruction to our vision far beyond its limits, and yet it was thoroughly substantial, composed of finely attenuated and spiritually sublimated material. I have so much to tell you that I must forego the pleasure of indulging in details, however interesting they might be to you.

"The presiding personage at our reception was a figure of tall and commanding appearance, with a benevolent face, dignified mien, and large blue eyes, that seemed constantly tremulous with love and emotion. He held in his hand a magic wand, which ever and anon he would wave, and in harmony with these movements the most enchanting sounds of music seemed to be wafted far out in the viewless spiritual ether that surrounded and enveloped us.

This wonderful fact baffles the skill of mortal pen and mortal language to describe, and you must be content with what is said as the best that can be said, so as to reach your comprehension.

"As I caught the eye of this great presiding spirit I perceived the idea emanating from his mind, 'I am glad to meet you,' yet not one of these words was spoken. I essayed to answer to express my thankfulness for his friendly recognition of us, and I found I could not speak audibly, but my thought he caught immediately, and bowed in acknowledgment. He had been many thousands of years before a sage and philosopher on the planet Mars, and bore about the same relation to his people as Mahomet, Confucius, Jesus, Swedenborg and others of their day have in your world; and he is pre-eminent in music. All the great spirits of Mars are eminent musicians. Music, intellectual expansion and spiritual growth seem to be wedded, and go hand in hand together. These are wonderful relations, but nevertheless are true.

"In my next I will introduce you to some of the societies and cities of the planet, to be followed from time to time by revelations that can not fail to impress you with the greatest interest, and not only be interesting and instructive, but will be of great value to you in your after life in the spheres. My clear and venerable friend, be of good cheer, and in the sweet bye and bye I will accompany you on this very tour, and then you will perceive the difficulties in the way of giving a description so as to be understood by mortals.

"March 27. After the ceremonies of reception, the details of which, fully set forth, would fill a large volume, we set out under the escort of a select delegation of forty-seven in number on a tour of inspection, a few only of the incidents of which I can imperfectly touch. Many things observed by us I am not at liberty to mention, for the all-sufficient reason that you would not understand them and the world is not prepared to receive them.

"Our first visit was to a society of literary celebrities, located in a city of marvelous beauty. For our present use we will call the place the City of Learning, and the society, the Society of the Literati. These names are not the real ones, but serve our purpose fully as well, indeed much better. The city is located on the border of a vast expanse of water of a golden hue, and this limpid stream is a vast musical organ of sounds, whose very vibrations, as its currents flow along, disturb the surrounding atmosphere, resulting in the production of harmonies in musical intonations, not only delightfully enrapturing, but far beyond the power of portrayal in human speech. We stood upon its brink, and were enchanted by its soul-piercing melody. Ever and anon the mellowed rays of the spiritual sun of our solar system would strike upon the bosom of this majestic stream, producing in their rebound such marvelous, scintillating reflections as to cause the beautiful tints of your rainbow to pale into utter insignificance in comparison. You must elaborate in your own mind these feeble touches of my pen, for I can not stop to give minute delineations, but only the idea, and you can carry it onward in your imagination without fear of overdoing the picture or exaggerating the facts.

"The ladies and gentlemen composing the Society of the Literati of this one city are numbered by the many thousands, with vast numbers of co-operating branches in as many different localities. We are told that there exist still higher branches, which we were not spiritually fitted to visit and comprehend. We, as spirits from earth, lacked planetary development, but we have the promise in the infinite justice of God's eternal laws that in time, though very far distant, our earth, with its encircling spiritual spheres, will reach unto the gorgeous grandeur of Mars. Here let us pause and reflect.

"March 29. Herein may be found ample food for study, inspiring elements for reflection:

"*First*—How almighty is God, yet puny man is wondering whether there is a God.

"*Second*—How grand and noble may all his children become.

"*Third*—How patiently does God, through inflexible and unerring law, work out such stupendous results.

"*Fourth*—Man while in the flesh would arrogate unto himself the attributes of a God, when in truth it requires ages of effort and progress only to disclose to him that yet he is not yet an angel. But still how grand are the possibilities before man, inviting him onward. They can not be fully conceived by the finite mind, much less described.

"We saw many translucent streams, whose pellucid waters were charming to behold. There is a law appertaining to all advanced spiritual intelligences that induces the profoundest meditation, the sublimest adoration, when beholding, although only partially, the infinite variety and splendors of the creation; and I must occasionally pause in my narrative to give expression to this law of my soul.

"We were next conducted to a vast building, wherein was deposited the grandest library of books, and they were simply collections on scientific subjects alone. Elsewhere were vast collections on other subjects not intimately connected with science—books as tangible and objective to us as the slate on which I am writing is to your touch and sight. Mr. Swedenborg, being naturally of a scientific turn of mind, became absorbingly interested in this department, and it was with reluctance he took his departure therefrom. He made arrangements to return to study some things to be found here and which he has not been able to find elsewhere. He is promised aid by the members of the Society of the Literati.

"We then visited an assembly of representative men, and I am now about to tell you something that will surprise you, but it is nevertheless true. When I use the expression representative men I mean that each planet has representatives to every other planet in the solar system. I must reserve the next sitting for a description of the grand system of planetary diplomacy—envoys extraordinary or ministers plenipotentiary, as you would call them. The power is too nearly exhausted to enter upon the subject at this sitting. We notify you now that by these ministrations and recitals you are living many, many years in advance of this age of your planet.

"April 3. In your solar system you only claim eight planets, exclusive of the Asteroids between Mars and Jupiter, but the truth is there are thirteen in number; five of them have long since passed into their spiritual orbits, and consequently are not objective to your telescopes, and this state is to be the ultimate of all planets. Every planet, including the earth, is continually undergoing change, that is to say, gradually passing from the gross to the more refined, and by a continually advancing series of geologic and progressive changes from the lower to the higher, from the crude to the more refined, from the material toward the spiritual, all will ultimately in time pass into spiritual conditions or orbits. But as this theme is scientific, and not directly in the line of or pertinent to my narrative, I will abandon it, at least for the present.

"In my last I told you that each planet was favored with representatives from every other planet in our system, and it is from this system, spiritually originating, that you have derived your system of international representation. I do not mean that any spirit communicated this to the nations, but that in the early formation of nationalities and the commercial intercourse between nations, susceptible public men, by reason of their exceeding impressibility, got the inspiration from surrounding spiritual influences, and to a certain degree and extent carried it into execution in the establishment of ambassadorial relations between friendly governmental powers. But there is a marked difference between your nations and the spiritual worlds in the objects and purposes of such system. In the spiritual worlds representatives are deputed one to the other for an entirely different purpose from yours in sending ministers to England, France, Russia, etc. Your accredited agents of government abroad are simply spies to watch other countries, lest some trivial advantage may be gained against you in some minor and unimportant matter. Selfishness is the law by which they are to be governed. They are expected to be, and generally are, lorded and feasted, dined and wined, all in the high-sounding names of civilization and national urbanity. Ours are sent on an entirely different mission—to gather knowledge for the benefit of all. Our public and representative men are not engaged in learning the rules and laws of the stock market, how to manipulate it and how to create corners in the bountiful productions vouchsafed by the Infinite, nor how to secure safe investments with large and profitable margins, but to learn the laws of the planets, to the end that they may be utilized in the development and progress of their varied and numerous peoples. Through whatever other planets, farther advanced than ours—have passed, we, too, must pass, and hence by our representative spirits learning of their varied progressive experiences, they are enabled to prepare for and assist in the changes that must inevitably ensue.

"I can not carry my thought further than to say in addition that our solar system, as a system in its entirety, has representatives to thousands of other solar systems revolving in space, circling around their respective central suns. You perceive that the grandeur of creative glory is looming up before us in majestic proportions, far beyond our power to comprehend and portray. We look forward with great pleasure to each succeeding meeting, when we hope to continue our narrative if conditions continue to favor us.

"April 6. After feasting in the examination of the library of the Society of the Literati I felt an intense desire to learn something in regard to the religious teachings on the planet in its past, as applied to the embodied Marsians, in the curious desire to find out whether their theological and religious history bore any resemblance to ours, and if dissimilar, wherein by contrast the dissimilarity consisted. Of course, in the very nature of things, this opened up a wide field of investigation, and I can only give you points condensed and with the utmost brevity, and without any attempt at elaboration. As I have already informed you, the denizens of Mars do not use our language or mode of speech, and therefore I am compelled to transfer their thoughts into our language, and you must consider that much will be lost in the transmission.

"The planet Mars, in point of time, is much older than the earth, and consequently has passed through many more changes; these successive changes or epochs have had their respective theologies, and I was utterly surprised to learn that in some respects they resembled ours—that is to say, their earlier theology—the later and truer has no resemblance whatever to ours or any that we have had in the past. The people of Mars in the dim and distant ages of the bygone have had many gods and many bibles. Their older books or bibles are now treasured as simple curiosities belonging to the infancy of the race, and the wonder now is how it was possible at any period of their history that a people could be found seemingly so hopelessly ignorant as to believe them. The same fate, my friend, awaits your Bibles, Korans, Zend-Avestas, etc. But in all their speculations in religion they were never taught to believe that their remote ancestors had fallen from an imaginary state of perfection, nor that somebody else's sufferings and death were imperatively necessary to extricate them from the peril, and to reinstate them into the loving esteem and saving grace of their creator. While they had many follies in their early history, they had none like unto our own. They never believed God to be angry and revengeful nor that he would ever destroy their own or any other world by water, fire or otherwise, nor that men were made out of dust and women from ribs, nor that fish swallowed men, preserved them in good condition in their stomachs, and delivered them subsequently and in safety upon the dry land. These silly recitals of your bible will be ridiculed and laughed at some of these coming happy days."

"April 10: If you could be instantaneously transferred to the planet Mars just as you are in the form you could not live a moment of time. The intensely rarefied and etherealized atmospheres surrounding that planet would not maintain animal life such as yours. Yet the time has been when beings more crude, dense and undeveloped have lived and figured on the stage of Mar's history. The law of evolution or unceasing progression applies to all planets and in a degree of unfoldment according to the periodic duration of time of each. Hence, under the operation of this inexorable law of the creation you can readily and with quick discerning eye see the ultimate destiny of all—that is to say, the utter overcoming of the crude and unrefined by the spiritual absorption of the whole, and yet this law that lifts the lower into the higher has no limit or ending. You can therefore see in the myriad ages of future time with this law, all the while actively working, how inexpressibly refined and sublimated will become spiritual beings and spiritual essences. This constitutes a grand revelation, and presents in contemplation the grand possibilities in store for man and the fittest of all things material. While the constituent elements are the same, yet in outward manifestation the atoms composing your physical bodies, and those in the form on Mars, are quite dissimilar. The same elements that exist here, either as applied to the spiritual or material, are essentially the same as exist in the remotest realms of the creation. They only differ in presentation or outward manifestation, and in the degree of their development and progression. Here is another theme for contemplation and study, and the fact as here disclosed ought to fill us with proud satisfaction, for the inherent elements and qualities possessed by the millions of worlds, revolving in the unexplored immensity of space and their countless myriad hosts of people, are possessed by our world and our denizens, only differing in the intensity of their action and the degree of unfoldment or approximation toward maturity—ah, a maturity that never matures. While the law of progression is infinite it deals with the finite, and as the finite can only advance toward but never become infinite, so will this mighty law of progression carry us onward and onward, upward and upward through all coming time, and yet will never cease from its labors or find repose. What a mighty destiny before and for man!

"April 14. In this and my next I will tell you some things that will surprise you, but they are veritably true. I am dealing with you in verities, however absurd and preposterous they may appear to the unprogressed mind. This is said, by your people, to be a remarkable age, and in many respects it is so. You are receiving some matter far in advance of the age in which you are living, but it will be properly recognized and appreciated in the years to come.

"On the planet Mars jails and prison houses for the confinement and punishment of malefactors are only historic reminiscences of the past. There are now no punishments inflicted because there are no offenders to punish.

"The doctrine of sacrificial atonement, with its retarding influence, was never taught to the people of that planet. They have always been taught the supreme goodness of the creator conjoined with wisdom and almighty power. God being supremely good, and supreme in the exercise of goodness, they have not for thousands of years last past entertained the slightest apprehension that any onslaught upon their peace, happiness, and future felicity, would be permitted. From this ennobling conception of God came the desire to manifest a spirit of devotion and veneration, and consequently at an earlier period of the history of Mars the worship of the people was low and groveling somewhat resembling, as I am informed, the ancient idol worship of the Egyptians and Israelites. At the present time the two worlds—the spiritual and material—of Mars are so closely allied and interblended that the spiritual forces are enabled to exercise a positively restraining influence over the conduct and actions of those still connected with the physical, so they can not, if they would, commit wrong, or perpetrate infractions upon the law of right. By reason of this high condition of development those passing out of the material form are at once intromitted into the higher conditions of the spiritual world, because they are fitted for them. All are mediums and subject absolutely to spiritual action and control. This is what your spirit world is seeking to do for you, so, if possible, to pass over and beyond some of the rough experiences of other planets, and your people do not seem to have the good sense to see it. On Mars there are no murders, arsons, robberies, forgeries, slanders, and other crimes and misdeeds, for they have progressed beyond them. Do you not perceive the sublimity of this condition? and will it not be a most glorious consummation when you shall have reached the same altitude of progress.

"April 17. Another subject of inquiry engrossed my attention, namely, marriage. I became interested to know something of the history of this people on this subject, and I found it to be an exceedingly interesting one. At this period of Mars there is no such institution as marriage in the sense you regard it. It is not an exaggeration to say that a very large per cent of your marriages are brought about as the result of the most unholy motives. Passion, lust, avarice, etc., are generally the impelling influences, and seldom is witnessed a union from purely spiritual causes. It is needless to say these marriages are not only temporal, ending with the death of the body, if not sooner by an unholy judicial system of divorcement, but entail a cruel blighting curse upon the race.

"The history of your own planet on the subject of marriage is but feebly understood by you. Enough however is known to induce all lovers of humanity to loathe and detest it as it has been practiced in the past. It is claimed that God created animate creatures in pairs, male and female, and that, as applied to man, he cemented a union of one man and one woman in the marriage relation, and that this occurred at the commencement of the creation in the Garden of Eden. Your conspicuous bible characters, such as Abraham, David, Solomon, and others, have not only ignored and trampled upon virtue in its simplest and purest forms, but with the hellish gluttony of the vampire feasting on blood, they debauched innocence, prostituted virtue to their unholy lust, and thereby destroyed the holiest relation of life. Their numerous wives and concubines attest this, and yet your pious Christians are waging a relentless warfare upon the Mormons of Utah and vehemently thundering against the polygamous practices of the Latter Day Saints. Shame for Christian consistency. On this subject your advanced thinkers do not discuss those eternal and enduring spiritual laws of attraction by magnetic and soul affinity upon which alone shines forth in eternal splendor the blending of soul with soul in an everlasting conjugal union. The people of Mars understand and adopt these laws, or rather harmonize and abide in them, and now while embodied their marriages are for all unending future time. As the result we discover on that planet a race of people almost perfect in their mental, moral, and physical developments, requiring only time, experience, and progression, to disclose the still more wonderful proportions of their being. The union of one man and one woman under spiritual conditions is the highest type of marriage, and constitutes the paramount and supreme intention of the deity, and is the ultimatum and consummation of the law of conjugal love—all others are fleeting, dishonoring, and only evil.

"April 20. Your candidates for matrimony, first obtaining each other's consent, and the approval of parents or guardians, apply to the legally constituted authorities for a license or permit to enter the holy state, and when procured they repair to a priest or magistrate, who for a few shekels pronounces a few stereotyped phrases, followed by the solemn declaration pronouncing them man and wife, closing generally with the ludicrous and farcical command, 'whom God has joined together let no man put asunder.' Oh, what a caricature and farce. It is bad enough to declare whom the law has joined together, and so forth, but to assume with such solemn gravity that God has joined in wedlock's sacred union many of the marriage alliances which are mere caricatures of marriage, is not only blasphemy, but the very apex of nonsense, and is the widest possible departure from truth.

"If it be true that God joins them together, no power, save himself could put asunder or disunite. To assert otherwise would amount to affirming that God is the author of failures. The difference between marriages that only have their basis in consent, license, and ceremony, and that marriage which God cements when two are joined by the divine laws of soul affinity and magnetic attraction—the one is of the earth earthy, the other is from the Lord through and by the operation of eternal law, and is therefore heavenly. Oh, that the children of earth might learn and conform to these subtle and glorious laws for their own good and in the interest of those to come after them.

"On the planet Mars the people have no license system on any subject. While you on earth are wrangling about licensing the sale of intoxicating beverages, on Mars they have none to license. While here you are exercised over measures of taxation to raise revenue to support the government, on Mars no taxes whatever are imposed, and public affairs for the general public good are administered freely and without compensation, purely as a labor of love. The truth is that the mundane affairs of Mars are more regulated, controlled, and conducted by the spiritual powers of the planet than by those in the form. The two worlds are so intimately related to each other, and are so closely brought together, that this is not only practicable but desirable and profitable.

"April 21. There is on the planet Mars a subterranean passage through it from pole to pole, which Mr. Swedenborg informs me he has thoroughly explored. There is more truth than poetry in what is known as Symmes' hole as applied to your earth. When the time comes by the settlement of your as yet vast millions of uninhabited acres, and a change takes place in northern temperature and conditions, the people of that day will discover within and through the very heart center of your earth a country nearly a third as large as the exterior surface, and by that time every thing therein will be sufficiently progressed and developed to supply the wants and invite the ambition and energies of the people of that period. But this discovery, or rather the occupation of this subterranean country, is very far off in point of time, and the human race of earth will then be quite different from what it is now. They will have so changed by the lapse of time and the law of progress as to be enabled to pass into the new country by way of the north pole with ease and safety. The north pole is the true opening, and can not be reached until the fullness of time, as I have indicated. As the area of territory of Mar's surface was about being densely covered by population, and apprehensions were being entertained for the future of the race, lo and behold, the new interior country was discovered and subsequently peopled. By the time it is crowded no more will be needed, for the planet by that time will have passed into its spiritual orbit and into the ocean of spiritual ether, where suffering can never come from lack of room. This will be the future history of your planet, and you will pass through the same experiences and reach the same ultimate. Behold how infinitely wise all things are forearranged. Just as we need by our development new limits, new appliances and new things, they are ready for our use, and are never disclosed until we are ready for and need them.

"April 24. At this time those living on the planet Mars do not die or pass through the change called death as you do here. They have no diseases that cause the untimely taking off of the inhabitants. Disease has long since been banished. All of the procreating elements of disease residing in the materiality of the globe or the surrounding atmosphere have been by progressive development eliminated. And even before this had fully occurred the people had learned the laws of health and the process of neutralizing and rendering harmless the lurking germs that remained. You may perceive from this what a happy people they are. There are no untimely deaths on Mars. Children grow up to manhood and womanhood; yet there is no fixed standard of time when all die, that is, no definite and invariable period of longevity. And right here comes in a great law, now operative on Mars, that the people of earth know nothing about, for it has never been communicated before, namely, children can not die there. It was never designed that they should die here. Marriage being brought about, as before stated, by the grand law of magnetic attraction or spiritual affinity, and all diseases being banished and their producing causes annihilated, nothing but absolutely sound and perfect physical and mental organizations are imparted to offspring by their progenitors. You see at once the idea, for I must be brief—the children being perfect in health of body and mind by procreation, and there being no diseases to affect them after birth, death can not touch them, in fact can touch none before the time arrives, varying in point of longevity for the separation of spirit and body. None die before the full maturity of stature, and some live to be a very advanced age. After reaching complete development or stature, they pass out of and away from the material in point of time, according to the antecedent conditions of their varied being. Some arrive after maturity to the estate of progressive experience in the form sooner than others, and when this period arrives, whether it be at thirty, forty, fifty or a hundred years, they pass on to their ultimate and higher state of being in the spiritual spheres. It is known when each shall pass out of the form long before the event transpires, and all due preparation is accordingly made therefor. Your scientists have discovered, and rightly, too, that about every seven years the atoms and particles composing your physical organizations change and give way to new ones. But this is gradual and imperceptible. On Mars, at this period of development, the changes are much more frequent, and these successive changes determine the approach of dissolution, and instead of death in an hour or a day, it goes on perceptibly and without pain or suffering for years. Every change lessens the material composites of the body, and at each a nearer approach to the spiritual takes place, until finally the physical, by the gradual process of embodied sublimation or attenuation, passes away, and the spiritual becomes supreme. This culmination is equivalent to what you call death, except that there is no attending pain, no death struggle, and no physical body afterwards to take care of and lay away. The body, by successive changes, has seemingly vanished into nothingness and been absorbed in the atmosphere.

"April 27. We have been expecting you to inquire of us how the people live on the planet Mars, what kind of architecture in the construction of their business houses, habitations, etc.; what kind of food they eat, and with what raiment are they clothed, etc.

"You will have observed from what we have heretofore made known to you that the services of four classes of professional worthies have been dispensed with, simply because the people have progressed beyond their utility, namely, lawyers, doctors, preachers and politicians. Lawyers can only thrive and exist professionally in a land where conscience is not permitted to exercise its native simplicity and positive purity, and where the lower passions and propensities are largely dominant. When conscience, active, pure and simple, is allowed to manifest its functions in perfect unrestraint, and to act as the governing power in the regulation of human conduct, the presence and office of the barrister are no longer of use. Lawyers flourish as a general proposition on strife and contention, bad faith and unfair dealing; and when these shall happily end, like poor cashiered Cassio, their occupation will be gone. The doctors grow opulent by medication, because of the ignorance of the people with reference to the true laws of marriage, proper antenatal conditions, neglect of proper hygiene, and ignorance as to overcoming or rendering harmless the deleterious conditions, both atmospheric and from the undeveloped state of inherent nature. But when, by progressing beyond their harmful influences, or by enlightenment and healing gifts, the people shall obtain a complete mastery over them, disease shall be banished, then the avocation of the physician ends, and he will have to seek a livelihood in other pursuits.

"The preacher lives in comfortable indolence because of the ignorance and superstition of the people. His office is one of hypocrisy and fraud. Hypocrisy, because if he is not a fool, he knows his teachings are not true, and of fraud, because by dissembling he extorts from his parishoners a dishonorable subsistence. When the people grow sufficiently wise they will be taught by the denizens of the spirit world truth and righteousness. Then the mission or office of the sacerdotal gentlemen will be closed, and they can seek employment in the many more honorable occupations. The politician, cunning and subtle, swims along smoothly upon the rolling current of the credulity of the people and his own duplicity. He prospers because you have not as yet grown into full political manhood, and he succeeds in hoodwinking you with the belief that his heart is overflowing with patriotism and anxious solicitude for the public weal. But I must leave this class—the politicians—to the tender mercies of several gentlemen who are waiting the opportunity to contribute their part to your enterprise.

"April 28. The coarse food necessary for you in order to keep up the crude materiality of which your physical make-up is composed, is not needed by the denizens of Mars. In the composition of your physical bodies is a representative of all the material elements in nature—iron, calcium, wood, earth, etc.—and it is easily demonstrated by microscopic inspection and chemical analysis, that in every drop of blood in the human system all these varied and numerous elements are represented. Hence man may be safely considered a microcosm, or nature in her vast domain, reflected in miniature. But you still exist in the realm of the crude, and yet you are vastly more refined than in the ages past, and forward, onward, and upward is the line of march marked out for you by the infinitely wise director of all things. On the planet Mars no animal food is used, because among other reasons the physical properties of the body do not require the elements of animal flesh to replace nature's wastes. Thousands of former species of animals have become extinct, swallowed up in the ever surging maelstrom of progression or absorbed in the higher forms. Vegetation in the planet Mars is quite different, both in expression or appearance, and constituent composition from the vegetation of your planet. Here the aroma residing in the vegetable and escaping therefrom, is largely absorbed and neutralized by the grossness of the vegetable itself, while on Mars the grossness has become so diminished that to the senses the aroma has almost become tangibly objective, and this aroma is food strengthening and invigorating, is nearly sufficient of itself to support existence in the form without the assistance of the more substantial fibers of the parent vegetable. Yet in a certain prepared form the substantial material is used. The time is not very far distant, as I am assured, when the people there will subsist on aromatic emanations from material productions, aided by magnetic, electric, and other atmospheric properties used simply by inhalation. In the water you use are to be found teeming millions of living and moving animalcules. They are enabled to live on the elements of the water in its present gross state, but on the planet Mars the water has been dispossessed of its life germinating and life sustaining properties to aquatic productions, and has thus progressed with all other things and beings. No life or form of life is now brought into being there, but such higher types as are fitted to pass with the planet into spiritual conditions; and the water being so purified by nature's refining processes is as different from your ordinary water as clear, sparkling sprays projected from your fountains and dancing in the sunbeams are to the murky waters of your rivulets immediately after a violent rain-storm. I will resume this subject in my next.

"May I. On Mars they have learned how to produce from the soil itself any vegetable that naturally grows therefrom. In the soil itself reside all the constituent elements of all vegetation in their infinite variety. You may thoughtlessly answer, that in order to produce any species of vegetation used for table consumption, the seed or germ must first be sown in the soil beneath the surface, but you forget that this process is but the result of civilization and art, and that originally, that is before you learned how to obtain and use seed, the products sprang of themselves and apparently spontaneously from the earth. Whence did they come? and whence were their germinating and generating powers obtained? Think a little deeply on the subject, and you will be led irresistibly to the correct conclusion that in the soil exists all the requisite elements in the production of vegetation by growth. The people of Mars have acquired the knowledge which enables them to produce out of the soil, abstractly considered, all the essential qualities of the vegetable without waiting for the tedious process of growth. This process is purely chemical, and everybody there understands it. Hence you see they do not have to buy vegetables, for all can have their essential qualities for food without cost to the consumer. Long since the ownership of the soil by individuals was abandoned for the general common good, and on this subject the primitive condition of affairs in your planet prevails universally on Mars—that is to say everybody owns realty, one just as much as another. This is pure unadulterated agrarianism in its highest and most perfect form.

"It is often asked in your intercourse with the world of spirits: What are the employments of spirits? what are they about? what do they do? etc. It is pertinent to inquire, What are the employments of the people of Mars still embodied? What do they do since we have discovered that they do not now toil for the acquisition of riches, because they have no possible use for them;

no taxes to pay, no governmental machinery to support, no lawyers to annoy, no preachers to vex, torture, and maintain, no doctors to nauseate with their drugs, no politicians to hoodwink the people and feed at the public crib, no grocery bills to look after and liquidate, etc. Before we answer these and many other important queries, we shall see what the people do for raiment with which to clothe themselves, and what they do for shelter, if, indeed, shelter is necessary. If we shall discover that these are free gifts from the father, then the employments of the embodied Marsians becomes a question of very interesting and pressing importance.

"May 4. I suspect that you already anticipate the tenor of what we have to tell you in regard to the clothing of the people of Mars, what texture, how derived, etc. Your keen perceptions and astute comprehension enables you to see at a glance that if this law of progression, as applied to the material, whereby the lowest forms are reached and operated upon, lifting with its strong arms into higher and still higher conditions, be true, it must be true and in regard to all material things—the soil, rock, wood, water, etc., animal and vegetable life, and as we shall have occasion to show further on, to the mundane atmosphere surrounding the planet. All things progress and advance in like and equal ratio, leaving nothing behind or unaffected by the law. This advancing march of matter from the crude and gross into the more refined and sublimated is seemingly slow, but nevertheless sure and unerringly, indiscriminate, and precise. Therefore the raiment worn by the denizens of Mars has reached the same altitude of refinement as all other material things.

"The seasons, once resembling yours, spring, summer, autumn, and winter, have nearly merged, that is to say, have nearly blended into one perpetual season of summer loveliness. The austerity of winter, with its stormy blasts and cold, piercing wind waves has long since ceased to be; no frosts to nip and blight the fruits and flowers; no chilling autumns, with withering leaf, to inspire with melancholy and sadness. What will surprise you in this connection is, that, while the cold temperature has wrought its work in the development of the past, and is only known to have once existed by historic relation, the intense heat of summer has also disappeared. When you have severely cold winters, almost unendurable even in your temperate zones, your wise philosophers theorize that your ultimate destiny is to freeze out; that the icebergs and ice glaziers of the north are ultimately either to roll over the now fair portions of the earth, destroying all things animate, or that their freezing breath will sweep over the globe involving in death all the fair and lovely forms of nature's productions, including godlike man, the apex and crowning glory of creation. But lo! when the earth straightens up on her axis and the cold waves retreat and sink away in their northern hiding place, and the genial and vernal season with its pleasant temperature returns, these same philosophers take a breathing spell, rest awhile, and conclude that it has not been so very cold after all; and when the summer comes, if it happens to be unusual in the intensity of its heat, and the solar rays seem to almost melt into molten ruin all things, and to scorch the forest leaves and wilt the waving harvests, these same philosophical wiseacres change tactics, reverse their position, and with one heroic bound jump to a directly opposite conclusion, namely: that we are all destined ultimately to burn up and become annihilated in a general conflagration by solar heat igniting the combustible material of the planet and its surrounding atmosphere. Oh, how impotent in philosophy! A simple and humble inquiry settles the question. Why destroy this fair earth, daily and hourly becoming still fairer? Does God do any thing without an allwise and beneficent purpose? Is it possible for Him to do a silly, foolish thing? He would certainly not destroy the earth unless there was thereby some noble and beneficent purpose to subserve. What grand purpose, good and wise, can be accomplished by ending the existence of a planet that has as yet scarcely begun to live? To assume that He will do such a thing, is to assume that He has become disappointed and disgusted with his own creation, which annuls His wisdom and foresight, or that He delights in folly, making a world and then destroying it because He can, or for any other silly and insufficient reason. To thus assume is to dishonor Him as a God, and to invest Him with the attributes of a devil.

"Wonderful changes do occur marking epochs, or cycles, in the history of all planets. Where you live to-day, thousands upon thousands of years ago another race of human beings lived, attaining a certain degree of development in science and art, but upon the fulfillment of their mission they passed away from the face of the earth. Where you now live was once swept over by old ocean, and where the deep waters and angry billows of the Atlantic now roll and revel once lived a race of people called the Atlantians, but their land with its embellishments of art and progressive development became submerged by the changes of the mighty waters, and now lies buried beneath its rolling deep and lashing waves. But observe in all this that the globe goes on, and succeeding developments of man and material things come forth far in advance of the former order of things. What, if in the womb of time it is reserved for Atlantis to arise from her watery entombment and to flourish again with renewed and increased grandeur, involving the submersion of other portions of the earth's surface, including your own? This would not be death to any portion of the planet in any high and exalted sense, but a progressive change, a revivifying of life, a quickening and impulsion of being in the grand advancing march of development and sublimation. As we write, the theme expands and enlarges, and as the power begins to wane we find we have not discoursed minutely on the subject of raiment, and beg your indulgence for a resume of the subject in our next.

"May 5. There being, at this stage of development on Mars, no winter with its concomitants of winds and storm, snow and ice, you have no difficulty in apprehending that very light material only is needed to protect and render comfortable the persons of the people. Material of the texture of your lightest flannel underwear would be oppressively and uncomfortably warm, and indeed insufferable. Thin and quite gauzy robes composed of finely attenuated and exquisitely refined material constitute their apparel. I have told you hitherto that of the animal kingdom only the fittest have survived the marvelous successive changes in the infinite series of progressive advancements. Among those now living with the ability of propagation is an animal species somewhat resembling your sheep, but so exceedingly refined as to be remarkably striking in contrast. Of course, and in the very nature of things, the fleecy wool, or, rather velvety down, that grows upon this noble animal, so distinguished for innocence, æsthetic tastes in food and refinement in habits of life, is eminently suited for purposes of habilament, and accordingly is thus utilized. They are propagated in unlimited numbers, live to an advanced age, are the common property of all the people, and have within themselves the qualities of eternal being.

"The forest and other trees, shrubs and flowers, have advanced under the same law of progress. Very many species of the olden time disappearing—the fittest only having survived. Among those now extant on the planet, is a peculiar and quite extensively cultivated species, from which is produced a fabric resembling somewhat your cotton production, with the same difference in refinement of texture as exists between your wool and that developed on Mars as herein stated. This is utilized for raiment also. Besides the people there have mastered the law that spirits employ in the materialization of garments at your materializing seances, only much finer, and out of the ambient atmosphere, filled as it is with sublimated atoms and emanations, they are enabled to collect and magnetize into solidified form appropriate garments for their use and comfort. When thus magnetized into objective and tangible being it partakes of and assumes a varied hue and color, according to the progressed and advanced state of the person using the garments. In other words the magnetic aura and spiritual emanations proceeding from the individual infiltrates and becomes interwoven in the delicate fibers of the new garment extracted and brought into being from the viewless air, imparting hue and coloration presenting different appearances, whereby the grade or degree of advancement of the individual wearer is made known and determined. Here you inquire of the spirits to know what sphere you are fitted to enter in the spirit world, there they know by this means in advance of leaving the body. Your spirits in imparting light and knowledge to you concerning their state, tell you that a spirit and its proper sphere are known by the peculiar aura, or surroundings and clothing of the individual spirit, and this is true to the letter. But on Mars this law of spirit designation that belongs to the spiritual spheres of your planet, reaches out and reveals itself in the persons of the people of Mars before they have actually entered upon the spiritual journey of life in the spiritual spheres.

"Now the additional fact is disclosed to you that by reason of this mode of obtaining raiment the avocation of the merchant is of slender dimensions, and the manufacturer's art and pursuit, except as known and practiced by all alike, are now unknown on the planet Mars.

"In our next we will discourse on buildings, habitations, etc. We had hoped to reach this part of the subject in this communication, but as we advance the themes and subjects broaden and expand, and we sincerely regret that the power by this process—independent slate writing—although the purest of all, will not last us at one sitting sufficiently to fully elaborate our thoughts and descriptive delineations on a given subject. It has this advantage, however, it comes directly from the materialized fingers of the spirit without the direct use of the brain of another in transmission. Adieu until our next.

"May 8. The same reasons assigned in our last, why very light garments only were needed for the bodily comfort and happiness of the people of Mars apply with equal propriety, force, and truth, to the subject of their habitations.

"Your rains are produced by vapors, mists, and emanations from your oceans, rivers, lakes, etc., which by virtue of solar attraction or a reversal of the law of gravitation the vapors, mists, etc., are drawn upward in space until a certain density is reached, differing in altitudes of height, when they become congealed by the force of the cold attenuated atmosphere there into small particles called rain drops, and these are carried along by the undercurrents of uncongealed clouds until a certain electro-magnetic condition is reached, when the clouds begin to empty and rid themselves of their burdened contents.

"Now we have informed you of the progress the water of Mars has made in being dispossessed of its gross and weighty elements; hence there are none of these to ascend and to commingle in the formation of rain drops; hence none but the purer and refined elements of the water are exhaled and drawn upward, and consequently none but the pure and refined descend. These are in themselves comparatively light and of greatly diminished gravity, and therefore mild and pleasant in their effect. Especially does this become true as a resulting necessity, from the fact that there are no fierce winds or storms or cold temperature in the surrounding atmospheric belts or zones. The rains on Mars are more like your gentle dews of early autumn than your rains and showers. You at once take in the situation from this and preceding statements of facts that crude material structures are not necessary, even if the material for their construction could be found, and we have seen that such is not the case, for all things, including the material in detail out of which edifices are constructed, have progressed beyond and above their crude grossness.

"In some portions of Mars no structures are used at all, owing to the mildness of the climate and the total absence of inclemency in the slightest degree. In other portions the beautifully developed trees, and especially those that spread out their branches near the surface of the soil, are ample for the purposes of shelter. Still in others they have a sort of building which is a grand pavilion, embracing a vast area of territory, thousands of miles in extent, under the same roof or cover, which during certain periods of the year and day become luminous and transparent. The temples and gorgeous structures, cities, and magnificent edifices have been transferred in spiritual essence to the spiritual spheres, and have ceased to be as material entities, so when the planet passes into the spiritual condition outright and in toto, all that Mars could ever boast of in architectural grandeur and excellence is preserved and perpetuated with additional luster and beauty from the finishing spiritual touches by the Infinite Master Builder. And now you perceive that other questions come up right here and require recognition and treatment. Among them these: Do the people on Mars sleep? If so, how often and how much?

"May 11. Why is it that you require repose in sleep? In the infinitely wise arrangement of all things there are amply satisfactory reasons for every demand, every requirement, every manifestation, and therefore there are reasons why sleep is induced and is an imperative necessity in your present and past states of existence.

"When rest in sleep is long deferred from nervous derangements or other causes, your physicians administer narcotics to induce it, for they well know, as you all do, that sleep is necessary after intervals of wakefulness in order to protract your being in the form, and why?

"You have voluntary and involuntary functions or organs; the voluntary only, the involuntary never, can be suspended for certain periods of time. Your respiration and blood circulation are involuntary, and as long as you remain embodied in flesh will continue to perform their appropriate functions, whether you wake or sleep, for they are not subject to or influenced by the will. And it is by the unconscious operation of these that your voluntary functions when suspended in sleep are replenished and reinvigorated. You are, as at present constituted, made up corporally of gross material, which becomes wearied and exhausted by the active exercise or operation of the voluntary functions, and the nerve force will expend itself unless periodically reimbursed and replenished, and restored to its normal condition by the intervention and recuperative power of sleep. When in the ages to come your people lose this grossness in their material composition, your inclination to sleep and the necessity for it will abate and become lessened correspondingly to your successive stages of advancement in progressive development.

"Thus is revealed to you the fact that on Mars, at this time, the inhabitants have but very little need of sleep. They sleep, but in a modified sense as to periods, duration and manner. They rest when fatigued, and for brief periods pass into a state of languor or stupidity, to some extent analogous to your sleeping state, which is never required oftener than once a week, and then only for a few hours.

"Your spirit friends will tell you that they never sleep, but rest, and ever keep in mind that the people of Mars are closely approximating the spiritual. Then, again, on Mars they do not have night as you do, and consequently not the same nocturnal influences to suggest and invite sleep. This suggests another subject germane to our line of thought. In nature you find always two extremes, that seem to stand in antipodal relations to each other. Let us give a few instances in illustration: You have day and night, cold and heat, male and female, fire and water, good and evil, etc. Some of these seem to be at fierce war with each other, and yet what a delusion! This seeming antagonism is but the working of a law that shall eventuate in the production of the completest harmony. Undeveloped people, ignorant of the jewel-crowned truths, as yet concealed from them in the grand arcana of nature and the progressive sciences, laugh and sneer at the idea of marriages in spirit life, when the unvarnished truth is that man, considered in his independent and separate sexual relation, is but a half man, and can not become rounded out into fully developed manhood until consociated in conjunctive union with the opposite sex—not indeed and truly until the man and woman become twain, one flesh, or, in better phraseology, spiritually unitized.

"The day and night will continue until finally and by gradual processes the night is banished, and vanishes in the splendor of a continuously refulgent and sunlit atmosphere. On Mars this condition is almost reached, and the night there resembles the shadings thrown over the earth when a cloud passes over the face of your moon at hightide, and ultimately even this shall be no more, for in the spiritual spheres of Mars, as in your exalted ones, there are no shadows to obscure or mar the radiant light of the spiritual sun, and Mars itself is fast approaching this sublime condition. We must withhold what we have to say in regard to the seeming strife between good and evil for our next.

"May 12. The people of christendom have had it rung in their ears for nearly two thousand years that man is essentially bad, unutterably wicked, unspeakably depraved, and, worst of all, this horrid state comes to him, not of his own creating, but by inevitable and unavoidable inheritance. In our ignorance and credulity how we have wept over the weakness and folly of our first parents in yielding to the flattery and persuasive eloquence of the cruel serpent in the pure and primitive bowers of Eden. Our tears have flown and flown, with no gentle, soothing hand to touch our eyes and bid them cease; no voice panoplied with authority to speak to; no words of hope and cheer. We have been told in answer to our anxious entreaties for blissful hope and loving counsel that there is a superabundance of evil in us, and a trifling, insignificant quantity of good, and that nothing short of a miracle of regeneration can save us from unutterable and unending misery in the life to come; that without this miraculous interposition of divine grace, the little good that is in us will be swallowed up and devoured by the appalling evil of our sinfully inherited natures. Oh, man, how you degrade your true nobility, your godlike and divine nobility, by bowing the knee to this hideous monster of falsehood, and by kneeling at this unholy shrine. In direct opposition to this abominable and degrading doctrine stands the truth in its pristine and noble beauty.

"According to this Christian doctrine we behold in man a combination of good and evil, and in the struggle for the mastery the evil is to be mightier than the good. The good emanating from and partaking of the majestic excellence of the eternal, infinite God must, alas, succumb to and be overthrown by evil, its unholy rival. Can man conceive of a scheme more degrading and heartless, and more completely dishonoring to God and his infinite perfections of wisdom, goodness and power—a doctrine more utterly subversive of moral goodness, deific excellence, and that more completely wrecks the moral government of God and dumps into one common funeral heap the hopes and happiness of the human race. No, no, this is not true; it is false, false, basely false.

"What is the true theory of good and evil? Man, oh, man, hearken to the voice of truth, and be wooed and won by its gentle entreaties. Let the scales of ignorance and superstition fall from your eyes. Look upward for truth, and be baptized in its beauteous light, and cleansed in its pure and holy waters. Evil is the assemblage of elements in the concrete, if I may be permitted so to speak, and is simply undeveloped good, or good in a lesser degree. Evil is evanescent and transitory, good is permanent and eternally enduring. The fittest of all things in the grand scheme of progression only survive, while all else is doomed to perish. The good and the true are as enduring and everlasting as the eternal God himself, while the evil and the false are fleeting, unenduring, and carry within themselves the insatiate and unappeasable elements of ultimate annihilation. Be assured of this, for no truth in God's illimitable universe has been more firmly established on a more indestructible foundation. Good day.

"May 15. Astronomers will tell you that in their observations through the telescope the planet Mars presents a red brilliancy not observably characteristic of the other planets in your solar system, which they are unable to account for. Considering the vastness of the subject, the immense distance in space where the scintillating orbs are chanting their silent songs of praise to God, the difficulties in the way of observation, etc., the discoveries in the domain of astronomy have been fully as remarkable, important, and satisfactory, as in any other field of scientific investigation. But still only a very little compared with the immensity of the subject has been disclosed and some of that mixed and interlarded with error. Astronomy will become the greatest of all sciences when by new apparatus and new appliances the spiritual spheres belonging to the various planets shall have been discovered. This success will be achieved in the coming time. On Mars the people have mastered this problem, and I was surprised to learn that they knew all about our spiritual spheres from their far distant standpoint of observation, and that they knew minutely all the characteristic and inherent qualities of your planetary atmosphere. They have long since invented instruments by which they are enabled to photograph in minute detail and perfect fidelity of representation every material object on the earth. And you will be surprised when I tell you that I inspected Stockholm, London, Paris, New York, your own queen city, Cincinnati, etc., in a more perfect form of presentation than your artists can reproduce on canvas with pencil and brush, and at the same time I was standing in spirit in the immeasurable immensity of space on the planet Mars. I can not give you even in outline, much less in detail, the modus operandi of this achievement, and will only say that the rays of light in reflective power will yet dawn upon your scientists and philosophers as the agent of discoveries and accomplishments not now even dreamed of by the people of earth. I want to add right here a prophetic statement, which you may carefully note, that the time is not so very far distant when your inspired inventors will devise and construct an instrument that will disclose to the human material eye, to the astonishment of the world, your own spirit land; for let it be well understood that your spirit world has a real, tangible, objective existence, that will yet yield its rich treasures in scientific revealments for the enlightenment and progress of your race. In very truth the spirit world is the only real and permanent one, constructed by the infinite master builder for all eternal time, while your physical and material, except their spiritual essences, are but the shadows and temporary projections from the spiritual. Logically and metaphysically speaking, the spirit world is the pre-eminent cause of your world, the mere transitory effect. This being true, your keen sense hastens you at once to the conclusion, founded in reason and truth, that an effect can not be greater or more enduring than the cause that produced it, but must of necessity and in the very nature of things be infinitely less.

"May 18. A people so pre-eminently advanced in all that appertains to the sublimation of their being, and all that surrounds them, and in which they come in contact, must necessarily be exceedingly refined and æsthetic in their mannerisms, habits of life, intercourse with each other, and in their vocations and employments. In the very nature of things it could not be otherwise. From what has been heretofore said relating to the highly favored and inestimably progressed denizens of Mars, it is not difficult to see that their pursuits must necessarily and almost entirely relate to the realm of the intellectual and spiritual, as they have passed beyond the requirements and demands of that which pertains to the material phase of existence. Physical wants require physical exertion to supply them. Material requirements necessitate attention to and labor in the domain of the material, and this, for obvious reasons, that need not be stated or discussed. It may be prudent, however, to premise that when the physical constitution requires substantially gross materials to keep up and maintain the corporealities of our nature, we must look to the productions of the farm and the fruitage of the forest, and also to animal food, which are always in quality and degree in exact correspondence to our status or state of progression. But when we lose the constituent elements of corporeal being that belong to the lower strata of the constitution of things, we require something more refined and sublimated, and lo, always it is at hand to meet the exigency, for let it ever be borne in mind that the law that is incessantly and without intermission working away in solving the great problem of life and being, moving upward from the lower to the higher, is not confined in its operations to only form or species of being, but applies to and operates upon all, whether rational or irrational, animate or inanimate, and pushes all forward and upward with perfect and precise equability and in exact and equally proportional degree, none advancing more rapidly than the rest and none lagging behind. Thus, you perceive the infinite order and the beautiful symmetry of the great law of evolution and progression. Herein is necessitated varied changes in the value and character of vocation and employments, suited to the continued mutations of things in the endless series of progressive changes.

"At one period in the history of Mars the art of photography was discovered. Of course it attracted great attention and challenged admiration. It was regarded not only as wonderful but marvelous. The discoverer was almost deified, for he was thought to be endowed with something of the divine nature not discoverable in others, until the art advanced step by step, improvement on improvement, when the divinity with which the discoverer had been invested by the admiring multitudes dwindled into insignificance, and the very sensible conclusion reached that he was merely highly gifted and spiritually inspired, but altogether human still. Compare the primitive system of photography, limited as it was, to objects of immediate presence to that now existing, whereby worlds and systems of worlds are made tributary to its discoveries and achievements. Now, instead of the wonders of the art inspiring hero worship of the men engaged in its studies and who produce the wondrous results, a feeling of awe and veneration for the continually increasing wonders of the creation is inspired. The admiration is justly transferred from man to the creator and the stupendous majesty of his laws and works. On Mars photography is now and has been for a long time a favorite and delightful employment pursued by the many, for all have the advantages of it. Therefore the study, not only of their own world, but numerous others, constitutes a pleasant, instructive, and intellectually remunerative employment. Nor is this confined and limited to material worlds, but reaches out and embraces the spiritual spheres of each.

"Again, take the science of chemistry. It once only dealt with material solids, but now on Mars it has reached a higher plane or sphere, and the sublimated substances, still possessed of modified degrees of matter, likewise atmospheric and spiritual substances, come within the purview and yield obedience to its powerful processes of analysis. This is still and ever will be an instructive and profitable field for those aspiring minds of the Marsians bent on the acquisition of knowledge and the understanding of the infinitely varied and universal laws by which all nature and the universe are governed and controlled.

"May 22. On Mars the people are divided up into a very great many societies. The membership of these societies is not a matter of choice and volition. Here you have degrees of social society, and you say there are three grades—the lower, middle and upper. This is so in the deceptive seeming, but in fact you have many more, but you do not understand the subtle laws governing in their formation and diversity. You also have secret societies, into which you require the consent of a certain number to gain admission, while at the same time a certain other number may object. Certain arbitrary votes in number control the question of application, and by them your admission or rejection is determined. In your social society quite a different rule or policy prevails. In a certain grade or stratum true merit and worth are not considered of any moment, but wealth and pecuniary par excellence constitute the law of attraction. In other words, and what ought to burn your cheeks with shame, it matters not how morally depraved or utterly abandoned to all real intrinsic worth of manhood or womanhood, a large supply of the world's fleeting possessions constitutes the real standard of respectability, and the sure passport into the higher walks of social life. On Mars they have long since passed beyond and above this purely human, unspiritual and unholy rule. There they are known and estimated as they really are, for they can not disguise their moral and spiritual status; it is read in the look, the walk, the thought-words, and most potently in the aura emitted, permeating and coloring the very garments worn, thereby disclosing by shades of color the moral, mental and spiritual degree of advancement. You have an old adage, which contains a very great truth, namely: 'Birds of a feather will flock together,' 'like draws like.' Under the operation of an immutable law of attraction and repulsion the societies of Mars are formed, and this law, so utterly disregarded by embodied man on the earth, applies to and is operative in the spiritual spheres of all the innumerable worlds of the vast, illimitable universe of God. And this law of attraction and repulsion is indiscriminate and recognizes no distinction on account of wealth, social standing or prominence among men. It deals with spiritual laws and spiritual truths and spiritual things. There being different societies on Mars, formed and governed by this great and inexorable law of selection or attraction and repulsion, you see readily that their employments must of necessity and in some regards be quite different.

"May 29. We have endeavored to keep before you, at the risk of being censured for occasional reiteration and repetition, the great primary and fundamental fact that all things under the divine arrangement advance in the ascending scale of infinite and unending progression by regular and gradual series, and in equal ratio; but you must note an important fact in this connection, namely, that all do not at the same time reach the same degree of unfoldment—some a little in advance of others, and so on. The question necessarily arises, why is this so? We only desire to say in answer at this time that all do not start out on their career of animate being at precisely the same time or under the same conditions, nor with the same or equal antenatal advantages. This carries us back behind our mere entrance into physical life, through and by the laws of human physical procreation, into a domain as yet unexplored, except feebly, by mortal man. It seems to me if men could only perceive and understand the grand sublimity and variety of their antecedent being, they would no longer be blinded to the future greatness and glory in store for them. This subject, if you ever enter upon it, you will find prolific of vast knowledge, immense and perfectly astounding revelations. But the time has not yet arrived for them. The people on Mars, like your own, not starting out on life's eventful and momentous journey with the same or equal advantages, have necessarily attained unto different degrees of progressive unfoldment, and by reason of this are their different and somewhat differing societies formed. In the same circle, order or stratum of society on earth, the good, the bad and the indifferent associate and seem to harmoniously blend and assimilate. But this is not true in fact. The degree of perfection attained in moral and spiritual excellence does not govern in their formation, and they are therefore incongruous, unsatisfactory and transitory. On Mars two unequals in progression can not harmonize, for the law rebels, interposes insurmountable barriers, and will not allow it. Those only are associated who harmonize and resemble each other, not in the accumulations of wealth, not in stature, not in facial expressions or outward physical conformation, but those who are drawn together by a sort of soul kinship, of absolute union of soul feeling, sympathetic inclinations and aspirations, having for their basis, as of prime and first importance, an equal degree of spiritual unfoldment. Thus divided and separated, there are very many different societies or orders, each differing in development, inclinations and aspirations, they inevitably have dissimilar pursuits and employments, suited to tastes, wants and abilities, but all conspiring for the general good of all.

"June I. The people of Mars are not so large in stature as on your earth, nor are they as large as at former periods of their history. The process of progression in casting off the gross, and also by affecting the laws of propagation, has materially reduced the present inhabitants in their physical proportions. Their feet, except in the lower order, are either not shod at all, or are covered by a very light and refined material substance. The nearer the spiritual the people become the less they are affected by grosser atmospheric elements, and this is directly the opposite of your experience. Here the coarser the material make-up the better can the severer conditions of your temperature be borne, and the reason is plain.

"Here some are progressed, physically speaking, in advance of the progress of the elements, and therefore they are detrimentally affected and influenced by them, whereas on Mars a regular advance in development has been reached, and all things now smoothly and evenly pass under the operations of the law. After awhile the same law will commence to thus orderly and regularly operate with you when this difficulty will be happily overcome. The grandest achievement made by progression on Mars has produced the greatest result in the formation of the heads of the people. Phrenology here on earth is but feebly and imperfectly understood, although there is in it a grand and most salutary scientific truth. Here, however, as yet, you have the angular and uneven formation of the cranium, with its attendant angularity of temperament and disposition. On Mars the heads are so exquisitely formed and so harmonious in the external, and so perfectly symmetrical, that you observe and note it at first glance, and following this high and beautiful development is discovered a degree of wisdom and learning perfectly astonishing to a visitor from a foreign, though neighboring planet. The hair on these magnificent heads is of a fiber and texture resembling your finest silk, and from under a beautifully arched brow you behold a mild yet brilliant eye, beaming with intelligence and affection, and they can convey thoughts and ideas without the use of words or the intervention of audible sound.

"June 5. Hundreds, yea, thousands of years ago, the development of mind on the planet Mars was extraordinary, and you can conceive what it must be now. Many causes, of course, conspired and aided in bringing about this result. The natural process of development would have ultimately accomplished it unassisted by other agencies, but a wise and humane governmental system was adopted, originating in the spirit world, which constituted a complete innovation upon and revolution in previous systems, and which gave a marked impetus to the growth and advancement of mind, and which produced also a wonderful improvement in the physical constitutions of succeeding generations. That system consisted of a legislative policy of the controlling government, rigidly and unexceptionally enforced, which provided that all children born into physical life should be given up and relinquished to the control and direction of the government, and by the government reared, educated, and prepared for the duties and requirements of life. Elaborate buildings, elaborately and artistically embellished and beautified were constructed at proper and convenient locations, where at a certain period of gestation, very early indeed, the expectant mother was taken and kept until a certain and proper time after parturition, when the mother was discharged and restored to freedom, and the new-born babe was taken charge of, raised and maintained by the fostering care of the government. Between the period of conception and parturition, the mother was continually kept under the most elevating influences, both of body and mind. Her soul was kept enraptured by the ennobling influences of music, and such music, of which you as yet have no conception. This produced in the mother the desired condition of harmony, which had a corresponding effect upon the little one concealed from mortal view. Twice or thrice a week lecturers, under the pay and patronage of the government, visited these asylums and discoursed to the inmates on scientific, literary, and moral subjects.

"June 8. These discourses were not only designed but efficacious in directing the minds and hearts of the auditors into the most elevating and progressively intellectual channels, and left their inevitable and unfailing impress upon the forthcoming offspring. In addition works of art, rare paintings, and exhibitions of sculpture were at certain times presented for inspection, study, and reflection, inspiring noble thoughts of the sublime and beautiful. Artists of superior attainments and national renown occasionally visited these places and gave exhibitions of their skill in transferring to canvas, in an impromptu manner, their loftiest conceptions of the beautiful in landscapes, scenes, etc., which were of the rarest beauty of design. Books treating of the noblest subjects were placed within ready reach and convenient access, and the inmates read them with avidity and delight. They understood that they were thus preparing the new generations, as yet unushered into life, to take their places, and that their success largely depended on the assiduity with which they availed themselves of their opportunities. The government, as before stated, took charge of the young and trained and educated them in art, music, and the sciences, and the result was soon manifest in producing a race of intellectual giants, and distinguished for their ability in the arts and sciences, and the benevolence or their religious natures. And to-day you can not find a man or woman of adult age who is not perfectly versed in all the higher branches of learning, and eminently proficient in music. If a thousand of them could be bodily transferred to America, and with her exceptional advantages, and live, they would soon, by the sheer force of intellect, rule this world, and lift it morally and intellectually upon a plane that would dazzle you to behold. And yet, my dear friend, it is laid up in the womb of time that you of earth shall reach this sublime height.

"The denizens of earth may wonder at and disbelieve these relations, but nevertheless they are as true as that the eternal God is truth. They point to the destiny in store for the future inhabitants of earth, and intimate to poor disheartened mortals the certainty and greatness of the future, in which they are to figure in no mean way nor act no inconsequential part.

"July 10. On Mars the doctrine of discrimination on the score of sex was never taught, but the equality of the sexes has always been recognized. This indiscrimination has always been operative in employments and in the choosing of persons to fill official station at a period of their history when officers were paid out of the public exchequer for their services. Of course, at this time when office is administered without compensation the rule remains undisturbed. Your troubles, that is, many of them, in the present and past have arisen either from a misunderstanding of the truth or a misapplication of it and its requirements. Can it be rationally maintained that truth and justice require a discrimination to be made adverse to the female? If so, there must be ample reasons for it, and what are they? We are told that, comparatively speaking, woman is the weaker. Is this true? and if so, pray tell wherein? You answer physically, and thus you would establish her status in all other regards, by the rule of mere brute force, powers of endurance, and physical capabilities. Do you not know that the ox and the horse, for precisely the same reason, can largely discount you? Do you not realize that by this argument you are appealing to the lowest element of your nature, that which only distinguishes you as connected with matter, and which as we have already seen, is transitory and fleeting? Pray lift the subject upon a higher and nobler plane and then let us have your arguments and reasoning. Is man superior to woman morally? Now, if you are honest, you must blush. In morals, man superior to woman! We all know this is not true. And do morals count for naught in the scale of being? In what pertains to the finer sensibilities and spiritual pureties is woman inferior? If not, are these of no moment compared with mere physical brute force? Do women survive death as men do; if so, which will be of greatest value in the beautiful hereafter—brute force and physical prowess, which only have existence in the lower realms of the spiritual world, or those finer spiritual qualities possessed by woman in a much higher degree than by man as they manifest in embodied life, and which belong to the higher spiritual sphere of being in the other life?

"Beware, oh man, how you treat angelic woman, for the future will teach you many lessons, brought about by your arbitrary and utterly indefensible assumptions and arrogations, among which will be classed your illiberal and unjust treatment of woman. She is your equal, and your great weakness is in withholding it from her.

"July 13. In giving briefly and very imperfectly a sketch of what I saw and learned on the planet Mars I have been compelled necessarily to omit many things, among other reasons, because they would not only be not believed, but in many instances incite unfavorable comments, if not absolute ridicule. I am not unconscious of the fact that many things contained in the foregoing narrative, although literally true, will meet with unfavorable criticism, but I have not been writing to please or to avoid censure, but to deliver the truth, much of which I am aware is far in advance of the age in which you now live on the planet earth. But it has been thought that a little work of this kind would be kindly received and amiably treated by at least progressed minds—those who had inspirationally and intuitively drank at the fountain of spiritual wisdom and spiritual things; and, as to others, it was hoped it might cause them to think it possible, if not probable, that man is something more than a mere fleeting bauble, a mere creature of a moment.

"To awaken in man the consciousness of the augustness of his being, and the mighty destiny before and awaiting its development, can not fail in this transition period, when you are passing from old theological theories and religious systems into something better, higher, holier, to subserve great and lasting good. In this transition process the great effort is to be made to direct the great body of advancing minds into the right channels, for in many cases the tendency is found to be toward the cold barrenness of materialism.

"The question that is to confront you in the future is not in regard to creeds and dogmas, for they are passing away, but whether these few fleeting years of physically embodied life is the all of your being, whether death is the setting forever of the bright star of our being in the night and gloom of ended existence, or whether there is for man a glorious life of endless progress beyond the life and transitory scenes of physical embodiment.

"July 14. With this my labors for the present end. The effort has been more irksome than you may conceive. The difficulties attending the act of communicating are more numerous and troublesome than the world would allow if they were fully explained. But we have done the best we could.

"To you, Mr. Helleberg, I return my thanks and the thanks of those co-operating with me, for the patience, earnestness and honesty which have characterized your association with us in this work. Our blessings rest upon you, and be assured that your greatest reward will be in the happy land which your aged footsteps are nearing. We shall shield and bless you here, and crown you in the land of immortal beatitudes.

"We would be ungrateful beyond measure not to speak in acknowledgment of the virtues and noble qualities of the medium, through whose superbly developed medial powers we have been enabled to speak to the world. In consequence of our frequent contact with her noble and pure soul our first admiration for her has grown into the deepest, truest and holiest affection. Heaven bless her in all her ways and walks. Her noble band of spirits, tireless, indefatigable and upright, have rendered us vast assistance, without which we could not have succeeded in the slightest degree. They are capable, true and honest, and able to guard and protect their instrument, before whom is a great future career of usefulness, and she may confidently trust them in all things.

"To those who may read my feeble lines I bespeak that charity you would like extended to you. Judge not harshly, but with generous impulse. You are in the realm of crude materiality, in the tenement of flesh, influenced more or less by many disadvantageous surroundings, which are not spiritually inspiring or elevating, but by and by you will survive and pass beyond them. Let me entreat you to study and learn of the great law of PROGRESSION, which we have constantly endeavored to keep before you. In that law and its manifold manifestations reside all wisdom, love and truth. It is that law that assures your future greatness and happiness, and will work out for you a destiny, the grandeur and glory of which you can but faintly comprehend and know. You can not die. You must live forever. You can not retrace your steps, nor recede in the development of your being; neither can you stand still. Therefore you must move forward, onward and upward, forever and forever.

"Fredrika Ehrenborg."

CHAPTER XI.

COMMUNICATIONS FROM EMANUEL SWEDENBORG.

The following communications, purporting to come from the spirit of Emanuel Swedenborg, at Mrs. Green's, are arranged in the order of their reception:

September 26, 1881:

"I greet you; good morning. You hail from dear old Sweden, my native land. The same native blood that coursed through my veins flows through yours. For a long time I have realized that your thoughts have been on me and the doctrines I taught on earth, some of which I would gladly recant. In my day nothing else could have been projected through my brain, and nothing less violent, though more truthful, would have engaged attention or commanded respect. My writings, as I now see them, were a strange commingling of truth and error, though I believe with truth largely predominant. I want the world, especially my followers, the disciples of the Church of New Jerusalem, to eliminate, in the interest of truth, the errors and crudities that unwittingly, though reverentially, crept into my theological writings. The hells as I portrayed them I now know were magnified into undue and absurd proportions, colored and distorted by my own preconceived notions, and, moreover, largely attributable to the religious temper and theologic thought of the time in which I wrote. Tell your good companion and others of like convictions to discard at once and fearlessly my unwarranted denunciation against holding intercourse with the inhabitants of the spiritual world. I misapprehended, and, alas, misinterpreted the holy visions given me. I was allowed to see prophetically that the two worlds would be brought into close communicating relations, and I ought to have seen farther—that it would occur through and by the permission and co-operative agency of God and his laws, and ought not therefore to be interdicted. This has given me vast annoyance, and I am very solicitous indeed that this shall be righted. Hold fast to this spiritualism, for therein only can be found light and love and wisdom. My power to maintain control is weakening, and I must close for the present. I will meet you here again. Good bye.

"Emanuel Swedenborg."

October 3, 1881

"In my communication a week ago I referred, not incidentally, but purposely, to my followers of the Church of the New Jerusalem. It is gratifying to me to know that they are in the main honest, faithful and intelligent people; but I regret that they have deemed it proper to resolve themselves into an exclusive sect; for, disguise it as you may, all sects are more or less exclusive. Among the many curses that afflict your mortal humanity, none are to be more deplored than sectarianism and dogmatic theology. Do you know that in the most ambitious moments of my earthly career, much less in the lofty moods of my medial inspiration, I never dreamed that I was to become the founder of a religious sect, especially one based on dogmatic formulas. The affirmations of material science now no longer questioned that in all organized structures reside the underlying, all-pervading and continually operating elements. Disintegration, decay and ultimate destruction of the organized form apply with equal and unerring certainty to ecclesiastical bodies. Modern spiritualism in this, that it is specifically and rigidly scientific, clustering beauteously around the family hearthstone, adorning and hallowing the family altar, may be distinguished by its infinite superiority to all other systems, it having no creed to establish, and steadfastly repelling all attempts at organization, is destined to survive the wreck and demolition of all theological teaching standing in antagonistic relations to it; and this God-given, heaven-inspiring humanity, embracing soul-uplifting spiritualism, is to become the universal religion of mankind. I will continue to administer to your wants and remove the scales from the eyes of the people, especially my followers. More anon.

"Emanuel Swedenborg."

On October 17, 1881, the following communication appeared on the slate:

"The blessings of the most high God and the benediction of His holy angels and spirits on you and yours. What I most desire to say to you to-day is that since our last interview here I have participated with others in a discussion relative to a recent scientific discovery in the spirit world which, when imparted to the world of embodied man, will strike the learned savants of your life with mingled feelings of awe and consternation. Our recent experiments were exceedingly satisfactory, and the questions that remain open are, when, to who and through whom shall it be given to the children of earth. The general expression of our society favored some time towards the close of the coming year as best adapted. In this view I concurred, for many reasons. My revered friend, let me say to you to-day, with great and positive emphasis, that the year 1882, earth time, will be the most marvelous year of the world's history, and will be characterized by the most stupendous events in all the circling centuries of past time. In that year and the succeeding one astounding spiritual revelations will be made to the denizens of this earth, utterly upsetting old, effete theological doctrines, and mercilessly demolishing now considered well established scientific conclusions, and your scientists' tests, self-complacent and arrogant in their pretensions, and possessed most fully of the spirit of vaulted ambition, the creation of their self-conceit, will awake to the consciousness that they have been mere pigmies in scientific research, and that on many subjects may have been so superficial as not to penetrate beyond the mere shadows and surface of things. I promise you that when the proper time arrives for this disclosure you shall not be overlooked or neglected. Bound to you in fraternal relation of a common brotherhood, embracing in grand reciprocation the inhabitants of both the mundane and supermundane worlds, I am yours, devoted for the truth,

"Emanuel Swedenborg."

June 12, 1882

"If we concede for the sake of argument that there really exists a literal hell, as depicted by theological teaching, and which constitutes an article of faith in most of the Christian sects, we are forced to inquire (and it is a legitimate subject of inquiry from the assumed premises), Was hell made for man, or man for hell? and this involves the question of duration of existence in point of time antecedent. Whichever way we determine, and our determination of the question from a terrestrial standpoint can only arise from speculation and conjecture, and not from proofs, one conclusion we can not escape, namely, the malevolence of the author. If hell was established prior to the time when the *fiat* went forth bringing man into being, and was designed for his abode and accommodation, we can not reconcile the goodness of the Lord with such utterly unjust and malevolent purpose, because to concede this much admits the possession of sufficiency of power to have ordered otherwise, which precludes impotency and concludes the will and purpose to so order and arrange.

"If the creation of hell and man as arbitrary acts of the Deity was coeval, then the same conclusion inevitably follows, before and behind the act of these creations resided in the Lord the power to have differently ordered; hence we must assume that the simultaneous creation of hell and man was predetermined, and in accordance with the will-pleasure and purpose of the Creator.

"If, furthermore, man was first created without any reference to hell or any preconceived purpose or expectancy to establish it, and that its creation was necessitated from man's unexpected disobedience, and as the only proper means of gratifying the vengeance of an insulted God, then we unwittingly and in a very silly way declare the absence of foreknowledge in the Lord, and degrade him to the level of a puny, passionate man.

"To assume any of these puerile positions to be true is to assume that the Lord, however august in power, and the physical, mental and spiritual ability to order and to direct, is nevertheless a moral weakling, and wholly devoid of moral excellence in degree superior to the meanest of his creatures."

June 15, 1882:

"If hell exists, it is plain to be seen there was a necessity for it. If created before man, there was no necessity for its existence, for the Lord is governed by the idea of uses, and there was present no use for it. Will it be maintained that the Lord would create any thing without a use and wise purpose? It is the uses of things that so signally distinguish his creative and moral governments.

"If it is said in reply that when hell was fashioned and established the Lord had in contemplation the creation of man, and that it was to be subsequently rendered useful as a place of punishment for disobedience, which implies that the Lord knew in advance of man's creation that he would be disobedient, then, oh, man, you are surely in the hands and under the power of a merciless demon, falsely called God. If this indeed is the true character of our Lord, then truly may his weak and helpless children bow their heads in sorrow and despair.

"These teachers of false theology, these false interpreters of simple truth, these false prophets of a false conception, affirm that this appalling hell, offspring of a monster creative agency, is a fixed location somewhere, which they have the candor to say, they know not.

"The theologians perceiving throughout the vast domain of universal nature two confronting opposites or extremes, and that there scheme must fall if hell were left alone to be the final destiny of the entire human family, erect another falsity and construct another place or harbor for the sojourners and pilgrims of earth, and consequently they say that the Lord has established somewhere in space a heaven, the location of which, although a locality, can not be ascertained.

"The same questions, with equal propriety, might be propounded in reference to heaven and the same conclusions follow. Was it made for man or man for it? Was it made before or after man was made? Where is it situate; who go there and why do they go there, and for what purpose? If the theologians answer these pertinent questions in harmony with their creeds, they would make my friend John Calvin, who accompanied me here this morning and is now standing by my side, blush with shame. He now, as a noble spirit, pities the ignorance and credulity that characterized him in his religious frenzy when in the form, and the credulity and weakness of his followers."

June 19, 1882:

"The original conception of a literal local heaven and hell was a feeble monstrosity and far exceeding the intuitions and anticipations of its originators, it has assumed huge and alarming proportions. Originally it was treated either as a human created joke, or as a wild vagary of the imagination, and in both cases without even the shadow of a foundation in fact. But as time moved along it began to grow seriously in the minds of the morbidly curious and credulously constituted, and it found many earnest advocates and believers, and they were not altogether limited to the ignorant. Had this been the case it would have been harmless and short-lived. The poet in depicting the career of vice aptly illustrates the history of this conception:

"'Vice is a monster of such frightful mien,
As to be dreaded needs but to be seen.
Yet seen too oft, familiar with her face,
We first pity, then endure, and then embrace.'"

"I unhappily lived in a day when it had been largely embraced. Had I lived in the day when it was conceived and promulgated, or approximately near it and been possessed of the physical, mental and spiritual organization with which I was favored in earth life, I would have undoubtedly earnestly combated it. But in my time it had grown into prominence and general acceptance among Christian sects, including the Lutheran, to which I adhered before my spiritual illumination; and hence while my spiritual mediumistic unfoldment, mental adaptabilities and capabilities would not allow me to accept the literal teaching of purblind theology on the subject, I was disqualified from perceiving and promulgating the real truth. I endeavored, however, to do what the theologians have never attempted, namely, to assign reasons for the existence of heavens and hells in justification and defense of the Lord. The groundlessness of my philosophy and the impotency of my reasoning I was unable to understand until the lapse of years after my entrance into the spiritual world, and then only by slow and discreet degrees. Step by step only did I receive the influx of spiritual light and truth, opening my eyes to the truth and impressing my soul with the consciousness of the errors and falsities of my teachings when on the earth embodied.

"In the spiritual world we are not allowed to perceive truth except by degrees and interior growth, and only as we are enabled to outgrow and disown error. Our errors, whether of acts and deeds committed, duties omitted, or false theories, either taught or believed by us when in the form, follow us to the spiritual world and cling to us with a perfectly amazing and persistent tenacity, and this constitutes hell and it exists nowhere else."

June 22, 1882:

"In my philosophy of correspondences there was much truth, with here and there a shade of error. It was argumentative, speculative, and characterized by analogous reasoning, but not sufficiently intuitive to reach the full height of spiritual induction. But whatever errors may have crept into this department of my writings, they have been comparatively harmless.

"What has given me the greatest annoyance since my departure from the flesh, or rather since I have better understood the subject; and what has given me the greatest anxiety to have eradicated from the minds of those who read me believingly, are my teachings on the subject of the hells in the spiritual world. I desire here to lay down a proposition I know to be true, whoever may state to the contrary, namely: No embodied spirit was ever enabled, no matter how highly developed the organism of the subject, to leave the body, go into the spiritual spheres, undergo experiences there, behold scenes, hold converse with their inhabitants, witness events and occurrences transpiring there, then return to the body, bring it back into normal action, and then correctly and in detail and in purity of narrative give to the world through the physical organism of the body, what it had seen, heard, and witnessed, during its temporary absence. If it were otherwise, and the spiritual world a real, fixed and objective reality, all who visited it in spirit during physical embodiment, would on returning and reanimating the body with the returning spiritual influx impart the same information and recite the same story. The directly opposite of this is true, and settles the question irrevocably in the negative as to the absolute reliability of knowledge imparted by spirits while inhabiting the natural body, although permitted by the operation of a certain law which is neither wholly spiritual nor physical, but a combination of both, to leave for a short period its tenement of flesh. Even then the spirit entire does not vacate the body, even for an instant of time, for if it did life in the body would become immediately extinct. However far the *consciousness* of the spirit may wander away from its home in the material house it must maintain an inseparable connection with it, at least by a portion of the magnetism of itself. Therefore during its visits away it is nevertheless all the while connected with the body, and hampered and fettered by it, and more or less governed by its laws and conditions. It can not, therefore, on returning, and it has never been wholly absent, give fully, purely, and correctly its spiritual observations and experiences.

"When I visited the spiritual world during my embodied life I was governed by this same law and subjected to the same limitations, and hence what I related was not entitled to full credence and belief. So it has been in all cases of trance in the past, and will continue to be in the future for ages yet to come. In my next I shall speak of some instances illustrative of this truth."

June 26, 1882:

"As illustrative of the proposition submitted in my last I will only mention a few among numerous instances.

"The book of Revelations states that John visited the Isle of Patmos on the Lord's day, and was then and there in the spirit. (I should have used the expression 'entranced' or 'trance state,' or that 'the Lord permitted me to see.') While thus in the spirit or trance state he was taken to the heavens. After resuming his normal condition in the body he essays to write out what he thinks he saw, or so much of it as he is enabled to retain in memory, and call up after again fully controlling the physical body. He says that he saw beasts worshiping around the throne of

God, and that he saw a beast rise out of the sea with seven heads and ten horns; that a book written in heaven was handed him with the command that he eat it, which he assures us he did, etc. Does any one believe that these were veritable occurrences, 'that there were beasts in heaven full of heavenly love, evinced in worshiping before the throne, and that books were written in heaven for men to eat? The Koran of Mahomet is an improvement on this, for it was not eaten, but preserved for use.

"Now, I want to say to the world, especially the New Church people, that my visions of the hells had no more foundation in fact than John's beasts, dragons and golden candlesticks. The difference between John and myself, that is, the important difference, consisted in the fact that John's symbolic visions were explained to be unrealities, while I was left to believe mine to be absolute verities. In fact one was as unreal as the other, and only forcibly illustrates the unreliability of this mode of deriving true and genuine spiritual knowledge.

"Your own Andrew Jackson Davis is another instance corroborative of my proposition. He avers that he has been, not 'in the spirit,' like John, nor 'in the trance state,' like myself, but, in more æsthetic phraseology, 'in the superior state.' They all practically mean the same thing. Davis says he located while in the 'superior state' the spirit world proper, and found it to be in or beyond the 'milky way,' thus inflicting a cruel blow upon the science of astronomy. Astronomy teaches, and correctly, too, as every well informed spirit knows, that the 'milky way' is a vast assemblage or constellation of suns, worlds and systems of solar worlds, and yet Mr. Davis was honest.

"Judge John Worth Edmonds, in his earlier mediumship and spiritualistic experiences, visited the other world in spirit, and his description of the hells recorded in his work entitled 'Spiritualism,' was somewhat analogous to mine, and very much in harmony with it. His temperament, mental methods and spiritual development were not very dissimilar to mine, and he had been previously as thoroughly grounded in Calvinism as I had been in Lutheranism. So it was but natural that we should see and interpret much alike. Yet in final conclusions we were in absolute antagonism, differing fully as widely as the poles are separated in distance by terrestrial measurement.

"Truth can not dissemble nor assume deceptive garbs, and all seeing the same things differently, proves that neither could be relied upon, for if they had been true and genuine verities, all would have seen and reported them alike."

June 29, 1882:

"Since I have been inducted into higher light and blessed with the true knowledge I have been utterly amazed in reviewing my writings, resulting in the discovery of two facts, namely, their prolixity in matter and stupendousness in folly. It seems to me now as almost utterly incredible that in my efforts at the spiritual interpretation of the scriptures I should have written so many absolutely silly and unmeaning things. It becomes my duty, and I can not be happy without it, to make this declaration, however humiliating it may be to me, viewed from your standpoint, but the truth and the peace, happiness and progress of my spirit require it. No work was ever written but what an ingenious metaphysician might not twist out of its every paragraph an assumed interior and mysterious meaning.

"But, after all, I was fortuitous in advancing many ennobling and wholesome truths. In all that I wrote I take greater pride and unto myself much rejoicing in my assaults upon the Lutheran doctrine of justification by faith alone, and in my enjoining love to the neighbor. However, to believe in and teach the doctrine of love one to another, or 'love thy neighbor as thyself,' does not require an inspiration from heaven. It is the doctrine taught by universal nature and in-worked in the web and woof of human nature. To realize and understand it we have only to become even partially civilized and to commune with nature and ourselves.

"A great portion of my life has been devoted to secular pursuits and the study of natural science. I also possessed some inventive genius, and during my purely secular career I was always contemplating, by silent meditation, employing the latter part of my life in the study of the properties of the human soul and its relation to the Lord and human life. Therefore when I came to engage the subject, it was not a spontaneous impulse to it, as some have supposed, although it was immediately attended and characterized by a degree of spiritual illumination and inspiration. I did not approach the examination of the subject wholly free and untrammeled by prejudice and uninfluenced by bias. I had previously conceived thoroughly deep convictions relating to this subject, and I now know no amount of spiritual aid could have possibly eradicated them sufficiently to have allowed the presentation of the plain, unadulterated truth.

"Oh, how effectually are we enslaved by education, association and mental training. The man who can overcome them in the pursuit of truth is far superior in all that goes to make up true manhood to the crowned heads and pampered ones of earth; yea, he is not only grand and noble in the full stature of his manhood, but he is more—he is godlike."

July 3, 1882:

"I do not affirm the non-existence of heaven and hell, but what I would be understood as affirming is their non-existence as separate, independent and fixed localities. If you will interpret heaven to mean happiness, and hell its opposite, that is, misery, we can fully agree, for this interpretation implies what is veritably true, namely, that they are conditions, and not localities. As conditions they not only exist in the spiritual world, but also in the sensual or material, and apply to both embodied and disembodied man.

"It is related that Jesus said, 'The kingdom of heaven is within you,' and never was truth more completely and potently uttered. At the time he was talking to men in the body, and to *them* he declares, 'The kingdom of heaven is *within you*.'

"If he is entitled to credit as an authority on the subject, and Christians certainly will not gainsay it, then it is quite clear that heaven, being in the human, spiritual beings is as a locality nowhere else. And inasmuch as it could not exist in the human being as a location, for this would give us millions upon innumerable millions of localized heavens, one for each breathing human embodied man, to become destroyed at the death of each, which is too absurd to be seriously discussed, it must necessarily follow, and as clear as the sunlight of heaven, that whatever that kingdom may in fact be, it is simply and absolutely a condition. And we can therefore readily see that as a condition, different with every human being, owing to the moral status and spiritual development of each, it perpetuates itself as truly and fully as does the spirit itself survive the dissolution of the aggregated physical atoms and forces of the material body, and moreover accompanies the real man into the spiritual world. So with its opposite—hell.

"If this is conceded, and no Christian can deny it with any degree of consistency, for the moment he does he dishonors Jesus as an authority, then the whole foundation of a local permanent hell is swept away, and the loathsome superstructure erected thereupon falls to the ground forever.

"Heaven and hell, viewed in any sense, are opposites, and wherever they exist they must exist simultaneously, for some are in heaven and some in hell all the time, and therefore if the kingdom of heaven is in the children of men, so also must be the kingdom of hell, or it does not exist at all.

"With my limited power I can not elaborate this point, or even present it as I should like to, and you must be content with a bare and imperfect statement."

July 6, 1882:

"Before the mythologists of antiquity had constructed a hell they had on their hands a personal, individualized spirit of evil, known as the serpent or satan, and more modernly as the devil. Investing this mythological creature with all the distinguishing attributes of the Lord, save that of goodness, they must have a localized place of sufficient capacity, and properly arranged for the enjoyment by him of the fruits of his labors. Divesting him of all goodness *per se*, the hell of their creation must necessarily represent his newly-acquired condition of total depravity, for previously he had been an angel in heaven, and must possess the proper and sufficient elements to enable him to gratify his hatred of the Lord in the punishment of his children. It was but natural in that day that the element of fire should be chosen, as it was supposed to be the most destructive element in nature, and best calculated in its very nature to induce the most intense and excruciating suffering to physical and material bodies possessed of the animating principle of animal life. In their unspiritual and ignorant state they supposed and believed that the bodies in the other world would be similar to those in this, and therefore subject to similar effects from heat and fire. What a monstrous conception, and how utterly inexplicable that it should ever have been believed. Even John the Revelator took a material view of hell, and described it as a 'lake of fire and brimstone.'

"I was compelled, or rather impelled, from reason or from experiences sufficiently clear, in my frequent moods or states of spiritual exaltation to depart from this grossly materialistic view. While my hells were in the plural, yet I fell into nearly as great error in my creations. They were the progeny of imperfect visions, imperfectly understood and grossly erroneous in their relation.

"You have only to think a moment seriously to discover the utter folly of my hells, and I will only present one instance among many equally absurd. You will find in my 'memorable relations' that I spoke of a certain class of Jews and others wading through mud, quagmires and swamps, and being injuriously affected by them, and this for the purposes of punishment. Now, the conception of a spirit, composed largely of pure ether, wading in the mire and wallowing in spiritual miasmatic swamps and filthy dirt, is only equaled by the mythological conception believed in and advocated by Christians that a spirit could be effected to any degree of suffering by material fire and brimstone. Both conceptions are as false as God is true.

"In reference to the mythological arch fiend of mankind let us summarize: First an angel in heaven; then a rebel; then a war in the peaceful realms of heaven, instigated by this fiend; then the fall from the angelic state; then a transformation into a terrible and grim devil; then the building of a hell for his use, convenience and felicity, and then turning over to his control and malignant fiendishness three-fourths or more of poor, weak beings, creatures of an Infinite God, and you have fitly spoken a system that could only have originated in an orthodox hell, figuratively speaking, and by an orthodox devil, and which for malevolence far exceeds any thing ever thought of in this or any other world."

July 17, 1882:

"The bible makers having established a heaven and hell, with God presiding over the one and the devil over the other, were driven to the necessity of concocting a scheme for populating them. The God of their creation they represent to be possessed of infinite perfections and glory, and heaven the very ideal of grandeur and beatitude. One would very naturally conclude that in their scheme they would have so arranged that God would have had the first choice, and heaven the destination of the best and wisest of the denizens of earth. Nothing short of this could have so completely enamored us of the conception and rendered heaven devoutly to be wished for; but here the arrangement in value and superlative worth meets with a severe set back. One of the weak and frail points in the scheme consists in not allowing this infinite God to have his own choice in selecting those to become consociated with him in enjoying celestial delights in heaven. Human nature, by the fall in the Garden of Eden, became weak and subjected to malign influences with an inadequacy of repellant power to overcome them. The cruel authors of this system, while they establish their god in heaven, a far distant locality, and keep him there constantly occupied and absorbed with the music and praises of the ransomed few, turn the devil loose to roam at will, and invest him not only with the deific attribute of omnipresence, but also confer upon him the extraordinary power without restraint of assuming angel's garbs even to the deceiving of the elect. In addition they place under his authority and to do his bidding an unlimited number of smaller devils, whose services have been utilized by him in preying upon the peace and happiness of the children of this world, and in preparing their souls for eternal punishment and subservience to his will in the world to come."

July 20, 1882:

"To counteract this terrible invisible influence of evil no power of equal potency is furnished. They say that God's holy spirit in conjunctive co-operation with the saints embodied (they mean, of course, the preachers and good church people) is seeking man's deliverance and salvation. They confess, however, that this agency is impotent when compared with the power wielded by the devil and his invisible cohorts. They make Jesus say substantially that the road that leads to heaven is narrow and circumscribed and few travel in it, while the road that leads to hell is broad and the many travel therein, 'many shall be called, but few chosen,' etc., etc.

"If their system be true we are forced inevitably to conclude that when the creative energies residing in man have succeeded in producing a high order of intellection the devil straightway captures them, leaving heaven to be peopled without the presence of the great and godlike in mental power. It would seem prudent and wise that this should have been otherwise arranged in order to have rendered heaven reasonably and fairly intellectual. No wonder, therefore, that their highest conceptions of worship and gratitude consisted in keeping up around the throne of the Lord a continual musical concert, both vocal and instrumental. Such distinguished and illustrious souls as Washington, Jefferson, Webster, Clay, Lincoln, Garfield, Paine, Voltaire, and others, could not be induced to participate for all future time in such exercises, for their mental constitutions were too robust and great and their souls too much interested in other and more ennobling pursuits. This kind of heaven would not suit souls of such intellectual proportions, and the orthodox hell, if accompanied by suffering, would be preferable to them, because their associations, at least, would be intellectual, for the devil is said to be exceedingly wise, and all wise souls live and delight in kindred consociations."

July 21, 1882:

"According to the orthodox scheme, heaven, hell, and the devil, all go together, or, in other words, they are inseparably connected with and belong to the plan. Heaven would be the destination of all without a hell and *vice versa*. Heaven and hell are in antagonism, and there would be no strife but by and through the devil, and therefore his existence is a necessity to this end. God is too good to take part in this strife, and is either indifferent or too weak to avert it. Even when the war in heaven, according to Milton, was waged between the devil and the Lord, with relentless fury, he would take no direct and active part, but commissioned Michael his generalissimo. How could he now be expected to take an immediate and active part, even to save his own defenseless children. Earthly parents act quite differently when their offspring are in peril, and so do the beasts of the field and the fowls of the air. I am talking ironically only to show the utter folly of the whole matter.

"In this connection did you ever think why it is that the devil is continually seeking the moral overthrow and eternal ruin of the human family? It is not because he has any ill feeling for cause against the children of men. They have never given him any occasion, and as we have seen, in their helpless condition, they could not if they would. According to the bible and the claims of Christians they have always done just as the devil wanted them to. He wanted Adam and Eve to eat the apple and they did so. He wanted Abraham to debauch Hagar, and after her ruin to turn her loose with her helpless babe on her bosom amid the wilds of the wilderness of Beersheba, and Abraham did so. He wanted Noah to drink of the wine and become drunken, and Noah hesitated not, etc. So in fact the assumption can not be maintained that the devil in capturing nine-tenths of the human family is actuated by any malignant feeling towards his victims. The reason lies elsewhere. We are assured by the bible theologians and their coadjutors that the devil is solely actuated by his intense hatred of the Lord and the purpose of wreaking vengeance upon him for banishing him from heaven and the angelic state. If this is true common justice and sympathy for the suffering of the unoffending impose most seriously the duty upon the Lord, either to conciliate the devil in the interest of harmony, peace and concord, and to save his helpless children, or destroy outright this malignant enemy of his. If he will do neither, nor arrest him in his diabolical work, then truly are we justified not only in withholding homage from him, but also in regarding him equally at enmity with our welfare and a party (*particeps criminis*) in causing our sufferings and preparing our eternal doom."

July 27, 1882:

"Why seriously discuss questions that are fast fading out of sight? The advancement of mind and the development of spiritual discernment are on the eve of relegating old antiquated theories and ideas to the past ages of heathen darkness, where they properly belong. Total depravity throwing its dark mantle over tender infancy—parent of the doctrine of infant damnation—is no longer taught or believed by enlightened clergymen and their followers. It only has a sickly foothold where the people are spiritually dominated by an ignorant or pusillanimous priesthood. Why, therefore, seek to revive by serious discussion any interest in dogmas now almost inanimate and staggering to their final fall and eternal sleep. Let them die serenely if they can, and be buried out of sight without pomp or regret. We have questions of greater moment and of much more value to mankind, and to them let us address ourselves. All things are not only progressive but eternally progressing. Must we therefore resolve that systems of religion and theological dogmas are finished and settled forever. If so, when did this divinely appointed consummation take place? It certainly, if true, must be an event of recent date. By whom settled, how and when? Certainly not by the old Romish Church and the hierarchy established at Nice and Laodicia, for their history since has been characterized by quarrels and dissensions, which at times have threatened their very existence. And certainly no one will seriously maintain that they have reached the high altitude of final and definite settlement by Luther, Calvin and others in their departure from the original faith. Some of the articles of faith of these have either been discarded or quietly abandoned, and those left have been modified, and are scarcely an improvement on the originals. In candidly looking over the whole field among the religious sects now extant, only one thing is discovered to be mutually agreed upon, and that is that man lives after death. We hardly need to stop to except those semi-materialistic Christians who claim that a future existence at all depends wholly on the physical resurrection of the material body at some vague and indefinite period of future time. This doctrine is so unscientific and so disconsonant with reason that we pass it by with a mere reference to it."

July 28, 1882:

"The Catholics have three states for the dead, Heaven, Hell and Purgatory; the thorough orthodox Protestants two, striking out purgatory; while the Universalists insist on expunging hell from the catalogue. Some will have one God, and others a trinity of them. But they differ materially as to the course to pursue in order to obtain the divine favor, holy unction and saving grace of the Lord. Here they are put to the severest test. It is infinitely of less moment to ascertain how many gods rule above, or how many states of the dead, as it is to know how to reach the much desired haven of peace and happiness in the eternal world.

"A prudent man would be comparatively indifferent as to how many ruling sovereigns over the destinies of man, or how many locations of consignment for their souls, so he is enabled to attain unto the highest good, and this consideration more imperatively absorbs his attention. Knowledge of the former would be valueless without knowledge of the latter. And hence in seeking to become familiar with the latter is where he becomes lost in the labyrinthian mazes of divergent and perplexingly diversified theologies.

"One would have you attend to the confessional, do penance and observe and conform to the dictums emanating from the Roman Pontiff and the imperious mandates of priests, thereby securing absolution from the consequences of sin, and due preparation for the next world. Another admonishes you that your salvation depends on the nature and degree of faith in the atoning sacrifice. Another that you must become regenerated and washed of inherited and committed sins by belief in and conformity to certain specific and definitely prescribed tenets. And still another, that a good, moral life is the one thing needful, Jesus having paid the penalty of sin and triumphed over it for the whole of mankind. And so on, scarcely without limit, do these various and varied systems present themselves to perplex and annoy."

July 31, 1882:

"Instead of there being one, two or three states of the dead, the truth is there are an infinite number and variety of conditions in which the children of men exist in the spiritual world with the qualification that they do not remain in them longer than they are enabled to progress out of them into other and higher ones. The plain truth is, as every intelligent and fairly progressed returning spirit will tell you, that faith and belief have nothing whatever to do in determining your status in the spiritual world, nor will what a man believes, however erroneous it may verily be, if he is honest in it, have any potency in preparing the spiritual conditions or assigning him his spiritual sphere. Here we must be clearly understood, that we may avoid both misapprehension and misrepresentation. I do not affirm that false beliefs and erroneous conceptions of the hereafter do not have any effect on the spirit. They do have a very troublesome effect. They do not, however, in the slightest degree, determine the spiritual status, for this is regulated by other considerations—moral conduct, noble acts, spiritual unfoldment, etc. But when the proper sphere is reached after death, for which the new-comer is spiritually fitted, they halt him there, and for a time impede and retard his progress, at least until he shall have outgrown false beliefs and conceptions while in the material body. A man may sincerely believe that the veritable orthodox devil is his constant companion, or that the air is swarming with malevolent creatures bent on his ruin, or that he is totally depraved by inheritance, and destined to utter and endless wretchedness in the other world, or any thing else, however absurd and untrue, and yet that man's whole earth life may have been justly distinguished for charitable deeds, love of the neighbor, and in all his habits, walks and ways all that the severest moralists could require, do you not at once see that in all justice and righteousness the man's life, acts and deeds must inevitably determine his sphere or spiritual condition, without the slightest interference by what foolish things he may have believed. And yet it is nevertheless not difficult to see further, that he must disabuse his mind of those errors of conception and belief before he can make any appreciable and valuable progress. And I tell you these erroneous belief and unfounded conceptions cling to the man with more obdurate persistency than the most of mankind could be induced to believe. Hence the prime importance of forming correct ideas of the future while still animating the material body."

August 3, 1882:

"Acts of charity and deeds of benevolence are estimated by the spiritual laws of our being in just correspondence to the motives inspiring and actuating them. By the motives prompting them, more than the acts and deeds themselves, do they become either valuable or valueless to our spiritual promotion and good. I have known men who devoted a lifetime of arduous labor in the acquisition of wealth, all the while wholly regardless of the interests and wants of others, and toward the end of the puny life, and in anticipation of the near approach of death, they bequeathed their accumulations to charitable and benevolent institutions, only to find themselves the merest spiritual paupers in the spiritual world. And why? Because being governed a lifetime by grasping and selfish motives, they only dispensed the accumulated results of the cultivated spirit of avarice and cupidity under the selfish and painfully delusive motive of enhancing their interests in a world to which their aged infirmity admonished them they were hastening. Upon their entrance to the spiritual world the motive met them, and overshadowed them with its pitiless condemnation.

"Had charity and benevolence characterized their lives all along for the sake of doing good and blessing others, it would have been quite otherwise with them in the eternal world of justice and truth.

"Charities bestowed only possess eternal value when done for sweet charity's sake, and with the unselfish object of helping others. This constitutes love and genuine love of the neighbor, and is consequently divine and heavenly and of permanent and enduring value.

"The Confucian doctrine, 'Do unto others as you would they should do unto you,' reiterated by the man Jesus, contains the great and salutary rule of life, which if practiced with the holiest and most disinterested motives will inevitably work out a most glorious future reward for the spirit. The shepherd kings promulgated this rule in a finer sense and reduced it to the fine realm of mind. The Confucian rule related to the *actions* of men, one to the other, but the other declares, 'Think of others as you would have others think of you.' If your thoughts and actions are governed by these rules you may conclude you are not far from the kingdom of heaven or angelic sphere. If you observe these because you love the right, you can not fail to love the Lord with all your heart and the neighbor as yourself, thus fulfilling the law of spiritual growth and development while in the temple of flesh, and insuring a condition of superlative happiness in the spiritual world. If in your present state of development you can not do this, you can, at least, make the honest and persevering effort to do it, and your reward shall be great."

August 7, 1882:

"Abstain from evil-doing from the conscientious conviction that it is wrong to do evil and right to abstain. Do not allow yourself, in choosing between right and wrong, to be governed by a fear of future punishment, or hope of future reward, for this is cowardly and pusillanimous and of no practical value to your future happiness. Do right for the sake of the right and not from the selfish motive of deriving a personal benefit. You have in your world two very injurious and reprehensible doctrines taught by learned men, namely: materialism and forgiveness of sins. They are both degrading and far reaching in their baleful consequences. Christians treat materialism with scornful derision, and yet it is just as true as that the misdeeds of life can be overcome and rendered harmless in their following consequences by death-bed repentance and the blood of atonement. One is as true as the other, and my presence here in spirit proves materialism to be groundless. Materialism is the doctrine of one world only, a mere passing moment of life, and suggests very naturally to make the most out of it. I do not mean to be understood as asserting that there are not good honest people who believe in this doctrine, but that they are good and honest in spite of their belief and not as a result of it. The theological heresy which proclaims the necessity of conversion, new birth, and regeneration (they are convertible terms) would be much more plausible if not supplemented by the more alarming and reprehensible doctrine of obtaining full pardon for repeated crimes and misdeeds just preceding or at the imminent moment of departing from the material body by so-called death. The first becomes bereft of its value, if indeed it has any, by the latter. It is tantamount to asking a man to liquidate an indebtedness now, when, under the law, he has ten or twenty years option. In a purely business view he realizes that the possession and use of his money for ten or twenty years is to him a matter of pecuniary interest and profit. So likewise is it with the man of the world with an organization tending to licentiousness and vice. He perceives no wisdom or practical use in becoming regenerated in the days of his youth, when in old age the opportunity is afforded to repent and thereby avoid the consequences of the loose indulgences and vices of a lifetime. Every villain who has run a lifetime unwhipt of justice and unpunished for his crimes, must be fascinated with this indulgent fallacy, while all truly noble souls must silently, if not avowedly, abhor and detest it."

August 10, 1882:

"While the Universalists are considered liberal and progressive, yet their doctrine is equally dangerous and untrue. Indeed, I have more respect for the others. They (the Universalists) claim to stand upon the Word, and affirm that the blood and death of one man propitiated sin so far as the future life is concerned, and that therefore sinning entails no hurtful consequences but such as are met with along the journey of life from the cradle to the grave. In other words, that the consequences of sin are visited upon us during our earth life, or not at all. They attempt to justify and defend their doctrine by a mere play upon words found in isolated passages in the bible, especially the epistles in the New Testament. The declarative assumptions of the bible, as translated for your use and guidance, are utterly at war with their teachings, and it is folly to deny it. In this age when the human heart and mind are reaching out for something better it is useless and unproductive of good to go back to the root of words in originals to bolster up a doctrine founded in error. The effort will always prove unprofitable and must inevitably fail of its purpose.

"I am aware that some advanced and more spiritually minded Universalists believe in progression in the future life, and in this regard their conclusions are better and far in advance of their premises.

"I would say to those, however good and pure, who expect to awake to consciousness in an ideal world of transcendent beatitudes without shadows and crosses that they will realize a most perplexing disappointment. They will find a world more natural than this, because more substantial and enduring, and what is more they will find they lack very much of being perfect, more perfect indeed in undevelopment than in that soul growth and unfoldment that would enable them to command the joys and delights vouchsafed by association with progressed spiritual beings in the higher walks and spheres of the spiritual world. To attain unto this state is the work of time and the reward of labor.

"The true doctrine is, as all shall know in time, that conscious and willful sinning, that is, where volition in choosing between the right and the wrong was within our power, is treasured up in the memory of the spirit and confronts us in the spiritual world, and will remain until outgrown and overcome by arduous effort. Happiness can only be enjoyed by the finite in contrast with misery, and shadows and crosses will fall upon us, marring our joys, until in the ages of coming time we shall so expand and grow towards deific perfections and excellences as to think no evil, thus not only rendering our actions submissive to the highest wisdom, but our hearts and minds to the divine love, and in a happy union of love, wisdom, and the will, we shall become something more than finite in our approach to the infinite."

August 11, 1882:

"Nevertheless let it be said to the humblest, struggle on, strive to battle for the right as you perceive it. If you see it not aright in good time it will be revealed unto you. Be of good cheer. You must needs suffer, for suffering in the right is spiritual growth—you are continually encircled by infinite love. You shall rise step by step, unfolding this latent power and that, gradually and by discreet degrees casting aside this harrowing and distressing memory and that, all the while aided by those spirits who have passed through tribulations and sorrows into higher unfoldments and joys, until finally you shall rejoice in blissful disenthrallment from the imperfections of your past being. Then you will be enabled to see why you have thus suffered and rejoice that it has been so. No pang will afflict you worse than those you have inflicted upon others, or of greater magnitude than thousands and millions have endured. Be kind and forbearing to the erring, be merciful to all, even the humblest creature of the creation. Deal justly with all, live uprightly, fear nothing but evil and fly from it.

Be brave for the right. Love your neighbor, which being spiritually interpreted, means all mankind. Endeavor to learn and believe truth wherever found; try, if possible, to think no evil; worship at no shrine but that of eternal truth, and no harm can come to you in the everlasting realms of immortal souls. No shadows shall darken the pathway of your progress other than those incident to your connection with matter and your undeveloped spirituality. And these shall be dissipated, facilitated, and accelerated, by the sweet memories of good deeds and good thoughts.

"In the feeble communications I have given you, by the permission of the Lord, I have not been able to impart my ideas in the same language and style that characterized my writings when embodied. I know they will be subjected to this criticism, but the difficulties of projecting my ideas into form in words have been many and great. If they were explained they in turn would be criticised with equal virulence. When coming within the radius of mediumistic aura we encounter obstacles great and difficult to overcome at their state of mediumship. Happily in time these difficulties will be surmounted. The aura of the medium and sitter blending with my spirit magnetism, your continued thinking and also the medium, thereby disturbing the equability of the magnetic and electric emanations, and to a corresponding degree affecting the psychic forces of the communicating spirit, and other things you would not understand if told you, all conspire to enfeeble the spirit intellectually, and, to a certain extent, limit it to the mental sphere of those present, especially the medium, upon whom we are so largely dependent. If you understood the subject as it really is, you would be surprised that we could even do so well. You, my dear Swedish friend, have aided us nobly; your motives being so pure and honest, we found in that itself a great auxiliary, and we sincerely thank you. I shall be with you often, and shall reward your many kindnesses by helping your sweet and interesting children in spirit life and others dear to you, to learn spiritual wisdom in their progress, and shall take a deep interest in you when you come to our life.

"God bless this medium, for she is worthy. In earnest supplication we invoke the blessings of the Lord, angels and spirits upon you both.

"Emanuel Swedenborg."

CHAPTER XII.

GEORGE WASHINGTON.

On the 16th of June the following communication was received, and those following at the dates mentioned, from the spirit of George Washington:

"From my home and congenial associations in the spirit world I come to you to-day feeling and hoping that I may possibly be of some service to my country, which I have never ceased to love with the tenderness of a mother's love for her children. Indeed, my country—the noble young republic—was kind to and considerate of me far above my merits.

"In the memorable struggle for independence I was assigned to duty at the head of the colonial army, and by this circumstance occupied a position that attracted to me more general attention than to others who were in nowise less meritorious. After seven long years of patient suffering, heroic endurance, and almost superhuman exertion, our gallant and illy-provided army won an honorable peace, and I trust an imperishable renown. A nation of freemen was brought into being, and a system of government established far in advance of its predecessors. The old Roman republic, grand in many respects and a marvel of excellence for its time, was still in many regards vastly inferior to our own. Being at the head of the brave army whose herculean efforts, exerted under many disadvantageous circumstances, eventuated so gloriously, it was natural, although no more worthy than many others who rendered patriotic services, that I should be chosen the first executive of the young republic. This, to me, was a most flattering testimonial of the high appreciation of and affection for the gallant citizen soldiery who so valiantly acted in the stirring and sanguinary events of the memorable contest. Regarding my elevation to the chief magistracy of the nation as a reflection of public sentiment as indicated more than as a personal compliment to myself, it behooved me by discreet official conduct and patriotic action to show that the general appreciation and esteem for that noble soldiery was not misplaced nor unworthily bestowed.

"If I have rendered worthy services to my country, either in the line of military duty or in the performance of civil trust, or both, they must proclaim my right to speak from my higher conscious life to my countrymen on matters pertaining to their best and dearest interests. If the gallant army that fought to a successful issue the battles of freedom in the infancy of its struggles here have claims upon the attention and consideration of the present generation, and those of the future, they beg you to earnestly consider the words that may fall from my lips and pen. I have marshaled those mighty hosts of noble souls in spirit land, and with them have recounted our struggles and sacrifices for you and those to come after you, and they are in hearty accord with what I shall deem proper to say to the nation through the much abused and little understood channel of human mediumship. You will hear from me in the immediate future in obedience to the purpose indicated."

June 23, 1882:

"Your complex system of government needs and will receive reconstruction or remodeling. When we emerged from the revolutionary struggle, and came to give the fruits of our hard earned victory some definite shape in the formation of a government for the new nation, we adopted the articles of confederation as the best we could then devise. It required but a short time to teach us that they were defective, and that prudence and wisdom dictated something different and better. The constitution was consequently fashioned and superseded the confederation, and there has never been any disagreement as to the superior wisdom of the constitutional form of government, at least, as an improvement on the original confederation form.

When this had been accomplished we were fully persuaded that the reorganization of the government under the constitution was the apex of statesmanship and the acme of the science of governmental construction, and were consequently happy and content. But alas, for poor human foresight. It very soon became evident that the new arrangement was imperfect, if not absolutely defective, and twelve amendments to the new constitution were proposed by Congress and ratified by the states. After and as the result of the late unhappy conflict between discordant states, or, rather, rebellion of certain states by secession against the rightful authority and sovereignty of the federal government, several additional amendments became necessary and imperative, and they were accordingly incorporated and ingrafted upon the already amended constitution. And now others are earnestly talked of and advocated; and does this not teach you the plain lesson that your system is still imperfect?

"The trouble is found to be that statesmanship is without foreknowledge, and is either blind to or oblivious of the requirements of the future. In other words, that the ceaseless mutations of human affairs, the ever acting and onward march of the law of change and progression, fail to strike the consciousness of statesmen or to secure their recognition. Of one thing you may be assured, your plan of government will be revised and remodeled to its vast betterment. When the time comes this will be most vehemently resisted by those who on all questions affecting the interests of the race and the happiness of mankind persist in remaining with the bats and owls of past ages rather than to be baptized in the light of the present and the foregleams of the future. But they must get out of the way of the car of progress or be crushed beneath its merciless and continually revolving wheels."

June 30, 1882:

"In the formation of your present system of government three co-ordinate branches were established—the Executive, Legislative, and Judicial—and they were designed to be checks, one upon the other. If in the zeal and frenzy of partisan strife, or under the baleful influence of venality and corruption, the legislative department should exceed its constitutional authority or enact legislation inimical to the public interests, the executive was invested with the veto privilege whereby the evil might be arrested. If, however, the President should be found to be in accord and sympathy with the legislative branch in its hurtful legislation, and gave thereto the sanction of his approving signature; or, in case the President exercised his veto power in the particular matter, and Congress should pass the measure over his objections by the requisite two-thirds of each branch, then and in either of these events there still remained the supreme court with its supervisory power or power of final determination.

"But it may be very properly asked, what if the supreme court should be influenced by the same or similar considerations as the other co-ordinate branches, what help, relief, or remedy, is left to the people and the nation? It can only be answered—force, revolution, rebellion. Does not this plain statement present a dangerous contingency and indicate a palpable weakness?

"It should be remembered that in our form of republican government all powers are derived from the people, and it should be furthermore very emphatically understood that all powers belong to them. If this view is correct, then in the hypothetical case mentioned for the purpose of illustration, the people themselves should be the last court of resort, or the high court of appeals.

"It was thought by the founders of your government that the judiciary would always be pure and safe, but unfortunately experience has taught us quite differently. It is humiliating to an American citizen, whether he be in or out of the body, to be compelled to make this confession. But truth not only justifies but demands it, and it is best that it be frankly made and acknowledged."

August 14, 1882:

"We are not permitted, for prudential reasons, to tell you how the new system is to be fashioned. To do so would not facilitate its accomplishment, but might possibly operate detrimentally by inducing premature consideration and discussion. Suffice it to say that the subject has been deliberately considered and the plan carefully matured by wise statesmanship in the realm of causation, and will be given to your world at the proper time and in the proper way.

"I desire to briefly discuss two propositions:

"1st. What are the duties of the citizen to the government, or what the government has the right to exact of and from the citizen?

"2d. What are the duties of the government to the people, or what the people have the right to exact of and from their government?

"First. The citizen owes the government affection and homage. This springs from patriotism and self-interest.

"Second. To render a cheerful obedience to and acquiescence in all lawfully constituted authority, reserving always and of primary importance the natural and inalienable right when all civil remedies prove unavailing, of revolution against and resistance to, tyranny, usurpation, and oppression.

"Third. Prompt compliance with all the lawful edicts and mandates of government. If they are deemed unlawful, unjust, and oppressive, first appealing to judicial supervision and all lawful means for relief and protection—revolution the dernier ressort.

"Fourth. Loyally protecting, defending, and sustaining the government when assailed from within or without, and when waging a just war upon a foreign foe, or in the suppression of an unjust and indefensible internal war, insurrection, or rebellion.

"Fifth. Aiding the government both in peace and war by being honest to and with it in official station, and by helping to uphold and foster its credit and honor.

"These comprise mainly the duties of the citizen to his government. He owes other duties to society and the local community in which he resides, but they are not considered pertinent or germane to our proposition.

"I speak of sustaining the government in war. War is a terrible thing to contemplate, and we would gladly crush it out in its every vestige, but you seem as yet not to have outgrown and developed above and beyond it, and therefore we are compelled to notice the subject, however painful and sorrowful it may be. The time is not so very far distant in the future when nations and men will progress beyond this horrible relic of barbarism, when the fierce god of war will give place to the sweet and gentle spirit of peace and brotherly love; when all differences will be amicably adjusted without a resort to the arbitrament of the sword and the instruments of devastation, bloodshed, and death."

August 17, 1882:

"In a certain sense the people are the children of the government, and in a still more important sense the government is the offspring of the people. If you ask me what, under the law of your present state of development, are the duties of the child to the parent, I answer obedience, maintenance, and protection. If you ask me the duties of the parent to the child, I answer maintenance, education, and protection. The family government was the first government in the infancy of the race from which all other governments naturally and progressively sprang, and their relations and reciprocating duties are much the same.

"I now reach the second proposition: What are the duties of the government to the people, or what have the people the right to demand of their government? It is the bounden duty of the government, under the constitution, to afford ample and plenary protection to the citizen in the exercise and enjoyment of civil and religious liberty. This protection is due to the humblest as well as the most exalted. The powers of your government are adequate to this end, if properly and effectively wielded, and if exercised without fear or favoritism.

"Again, it is the duty of government to see that public affairs are so managed that its burdens may fall lightly upon the people and mostly upon those ablest to bear them. A judicious system of obtaining revenue to meet the exigencies of government and the liquidation of the national public debt by taxing incomes on accumulated wealth and its investment in various speculative methods, would be most salutary to the attainment of the object.

"In order that the wise purposes of good government be carried out, and that honesty, frugality, and the most rigid economy should characterize every department of the public service, it is essentially and indispensably important that honesty and capacity alone should be regarded as commanding qualities for public official positions. Dishonesty and corruption and bribery in public stations ought to be severely punished, else there remains no safety and security to confiding constituencies. When your government offices reek with corruption and no alarm is manifested and no corrective measures adopted, you are not far from the yawning brink of the precipice over which your liberties and free institutions are sure to be precipitated. It is the duty of the government, in the interest of a confiding trusting people to hunt down the official vampires and parasites who thus insidiously prey upon the vitals of government, and inflict upon them such penalties as are commensurate with their enormous crimes. To allow them to go on with impunity and exempt from punishment is to invite and encourage corruption, and to suggest the safety of its increase."

August 18, 1882:

"It is the duty of government to foster, uphold, and defend labor in its unequal struggle against the greed of capital to the end that capital may not utterly crush it beneath its scornful and merciless heel. I tell you in all seriousness that on this subject you are approaching the verge of a volcano whose wrathful pent-up fires can not be much longer controlled, nor is it desirable that they should be unless a speedy change in the treatment of labor by capital, involving justice and right, is brought about. It is a delusion and in opposition to all human experience to expect capital, uncompelled by law, to become quickened in conscience and pervaded by a sense of equity and right. The government must stretch forth its strong arm and compel the exercise by authoritative and coercive power of a spirit of justice and fair dealing that belongs to a common humanity. Revivify and re-adopt that virtuous and beneficent doctrine of the earlier patriotic statesmanship of the republic, namely: 'The greatest good to the greatest number.' The men and women who toil and sweat in poverty constitute the greatest number, and he must indeed be blind to truth and deaf to justice who fails to discover or concede that the toiling millions have wrongs done them by the greedy rapacity of capital, and which appeal with vehement persistency for redress—aye, we fear in a little while, for retaliative and retributive vengeance. They have the right to claim protection from the steady and stealthy encroachments of capital whereby the rich grow richer and the poor poorer. Capital and labor are mutually interested in each others' welfare and prosperity, and are alike equally entitled to protection when dealing justly with each other, but under the present order of things labor is at the mercy of capital, and receives not justice at its hands. And this great government fought into existence by the common people, defended in every succeeding struggle by the common people, and which claims to be a government of the people and by the people and for the people, stands idly by with folded arms and with an apparent serene complacency permits the great masses of the people to become hopelessly impoverished, while the exclusive and favored few become enormously enriched. Verily has the government by its inaction and failure to interpose, become truly and in the sight of heaven a *particeps criminis* in producing this wretched and deplorable condition of affairs."

August 21, 1882:

"You have a tariff system, which for unrighteousness in the cruelty of its exactions, is without a parallel in modern times. It is unjust and oppressive; wholly indefensible, and with scarcely a palliating feature. My circumscribed power in communicating will not allow me to argue the question *in extenso*, or as I would like to. Your tariff is not only unjustly discriminative, but painfully oppressive in its operations, especially so far as the interests of the consumers are concerned. Why do you not honestly examine the subject in its bearings in the laudable endeavor to ascertain to whose benefit it inures. The government to some extent is benefited in the matter of revenue, but the capitalists are more largely the beneficiaries, and it is for them and their interests that you legislate. Have you not yet discovered, if not by close and analytical reasoning, at least by an observance of its practical operations, that the poor artisans, skilled mechanics, and other labors immediately connected with your manufactures, are not favored by high rates of tariff, and that protection to home manufacturing by imposts on imported commodities does not enhance the interests or confer blessings upon the consumers of your manufactured articles. Have you not yet realized the fact that exorbitant and restrictive protection fosters only the interests of invested capital, with no real advantage to the toiling operatives and to the oppressive detriment of consumers? If the operatives in your manufacturing establishments were benefited by high tariffs it would be manifested and plainly discernible in prosperous accumulations and in their happy contentment. The opposite of all this is true, and it does not require a philosopher to discover it. Why trades unions, repeated and frequent strikes, and an unmistakably unhappy condition of unrest, if the benefits accruing from the system beneficially inured to the workmen? The masses of your toiling people are inclined to suffer and bear injuries and injustice with a patience and forbearance not characteristic of any other people under the broad canopy of heaven, and when they protest by strike or otherwise you may safely assume that they are in the right, and have just grievances. The people not directly connected with the manufacturing interest, but who are the purchasers of its products, have exhibited a still more remarkable degree of patient forbearance, for they are much more numerous and less directly dependent. They have been sorrowfully blinded to their true interests by unconscionable politicians and political tricksters, and most dearly have they paid for their confidence and ignorance. We see signs of the awakening of the hitherto slumbering sensibilities of the people, and feel assured that in the not remote future will be aroused a sentiment among the masses that will compel a change of front on this subject in the meting out of even-handed and impartial justice."

August 24, 1882:

"Another subject of engrossing importance to your weal is the threatening and dangerous attitude of monopoly and corporate power. Your railroad corporations are assuming gigantic proportions, and bode no good to you if left uncontrolled and unregulated by law. Your liberties are not only menaced for many causes, but by this corporate power all the avenues and departments of your government are being influenced detrimentally to the general public interest, if not absolutely sullied by the corroding elements of corruption. These corporations, by the many influences they are enabled to exert, if left unrestrained by legislation, will control your government and its vast machinery as effectually and completely as the planets perform their circuits in obedience to the inflexible and unerring laws of the universe.

"It is nonsense to talk about the absence of constitutional power over the subject. Your national legislature has ample warrant, under the constitutional provision conferring authority upon Congress to regulate commerce among the states, and Congress should exercise that authority promptly and fearlessly. Railroads are common carriers, and are, when considered in connection with this power conferred upon Congress, public, and not private, highways. The Supreme Court of the United States has frequently affirmed this power as residing in the legislative department of the government. Unless regulated and restrained, these corporations may impose such exorbitant rates of transportation as to destroy ordinary profits on manufactured and other commodities, and necessitate an insufferable and unbearable increase to meet the exigency of increased rates of transportation, and, of course, to the detriment and oppression of consumers. The government must take the matter in hand for the protection of the people. Competition will prove unavailing without restrictive legislation; for the railroads would engage in pooling, and thereby render nugatory the natural advantages of competition. This monopoly constitutes the most threatening element in the country, and will be felt too soon, if not prevented by judicious exercise of governmental authority. The use of steam, as applied to railroads, steamboats, and steamships, was unknown to the founders of your government and the framers of your constitution, or more definite provisions would have been made in relation to the subject of regulating commerce. Why can not your statesmen be as patriotic and as true to the public?

"Although mainly chartered by the states, they are not authorized by implication or otherwise to pursue the selfish course of only subserving the interests of capital, but for the convenience and benefit of the great body of the people in commerce and travel as well. They have, by exercising all undue influence, corrupted courts and legislatures, and will, ere long, as they have already to some extent, invade the sacred precincts of your elections, corrupting the sanctity of the ballot-box, and demoralizing the independence of electors. Then your government will become a farce, and your free institutions subject to the whims and caprices of unholy and unconscionable monopoly power."

August 25, 1882:

"The great agricultural interests upon which you mostly depend for all of your material prosperity receive no protection from your tariff legislation, but are compelled to pay tribute to manufacturing by paying tariffs on manufactured agricultural implements used on the farm by the increased prices on the same. Besides, this great interest (agricultural) is at the mercy of railroad corporations in high rates of transporting the products of the farm to market, and in the end the burden falls on the consumers of such products.

"The recent tariff commission created by Congress, and its members appointed by the President, is a miserable subterfuge and sham, as you will ultimately ascertain. The dodging of the responsibility by Congress, of an immediate revision of the tariff and the correction of its abuses and vices, ought to be vigorously condemned. There exists no valid reason why the old war tariff rates should be continued in this era of profound peace and general prosperity of trade and business. Under the constitution, tariff taxation can only be imposed on imported articles for the purposes of revenue to the government, and this, however arranged, is amply sufficient to afford incidental protection to home manufactories. The time is coming when free trade and open, untrammelled commerce with all nations will be the policy of all wise governments, and the sooner it is brought about the better.

"The currency policy will also be changed, and a great wrong therein righted. The national banking system projected into being early in the late war, and which had its necessities for an apology, will be abrogated and done away with, and a currency furnished directly by the government to the people, without the intervention and agency of private banking corporations. This will be cheaper, safer, and more durable, predicated, as it will be, upon the good faith of the American people and their government, and secured by their prosperity.

"The time will come when the flag of the American republic will float over Canada, all the British Possessions on this continent, the island of Cuba, the natural key to the Gulf of Mexico, as well as over the cultivated valleys, arid plateaus, and towering mountains of the land of the Montezumas, beyond the Rio Grande. Then will your system of government be remodeled and reconstructed upon a plan infinitely superior to your present one, and the United States will not only become the greatest nation the earth has ever known, but the nucleus around which, in time, all other nations will cluster and revolve, shouting the anthem of human equality and freedom and universal liberty.

"G. Washington."

CHAPTER XIII.

COMMUNICATION FROM MY SON EMIL ABOUT EX-PRESIDENT GARFIELD—GREETINGS FROM MADAM EHRENBORG—LETTER FROM REV. GODDARD, AND SWEDENBORG'S ANSWER.

On the 26th of September, 1881, at the hour of 9 o'clock, forenoon, it being the same memorable day on which the body of the late lamented Garfield was buried, I went to Mrs. Green, 309 Longworth street, for an independent slate-writing seance. I had previously prepared the following paper, which I laid on the table, writing downwards, and which Mrs. Green had no means of reading, viz:

"Will our dear exalted spirit friends be so kind as to give us some information of James A. Garfield, our late beloved President."

On the slate soon came the following, signed Emil, the name of my spirit son.

"Good morning, dear papa. Many spirits are here to greet you. Our beloved and martyr President's work has just begun. He awoke immediately to consciousness and to the reality of a future life, of which he had slight knowledge. He was met by Washington, the father of his country, and the martyr Lincoln, with a crown prepared for him, and with many other loving kindred spirits, who had gone before to prepare for his reception, and it was the grandest one he ever had. He has been introduced to our spiritual congress, where he will finish his work, and where he will be more useful to his country. You will soon see a communication from the President in the papers."

Then immediately came:

"Dear papa, weep not for those who pass from this to higher spheres. Think of them free from sorrow and pain, and wipe away your tears.

"Emil."

Oct. 10. Through Mrs. Green. "My highly esteemed friend, good morning. Baron Swedenborg is prevented from meeting you to-day by reason of a called special session of the scientific institute or harmonial order of savants, of which he is a prominent member. Matters of transcendent import and pressing moment now engross the attention of that honorable body of advanced spiritual minds. He requested me to thus announce his enforced absence to-day, and to say that it will afford him pleasure to be with you at your next sitting. I avail myself of this opportunity, by the kind permission of the mediums' guides, to give my blessings, and to again urge you to go on with your investigations, and to push forward the noble work set before you by the spirit world. The elements for your spiritual unfoldment are constantly at work, and will continue to work out for you a rich reward far exceeding your most confident anticipations. Only fully co-operate with these elements and continue to act conjointly with your spirit friends and all will be well.

"Bright spirits of light around you stand,
Whom you have attracted from the summerland;
They come to bless you with their spirit light,
And make your life all beauteous and bright.

"Press forward, then, with fearless tread,
And learn from those the world call dead;
The veil is rent, their presence ever near,
Your soul to bless and heart to cheer.

"Fredrika Ehrenborg."

The communications from Swedenborg of the 8th of September, 1881, through Mrs. Jennie McKee (the first one from him), and those through Mrs. Green of the 26th of September and 3d of October, 1881, I had printed in a small pamphlet, and sent them to divers parties, and one to the Rev. John Goddard, a minister of the New Church in Cincinnati, with the hope that he would afford the members of his congregation the opportunity to read them. In answer, I received the following reply from Mr. Goddard, viz:

"Price's Hill, *August 19, 1881.*

"*Dear Mr. Helleberg*: Your communication with your pamphlet came to me to-day. I hardly know what to say in reply, for I fear that nothing I can say will be of any use. I have no doubt in the world that there is such a thing as communication with spirits, nor has any intelligent and well informed New Churchman. Nor have I any doubt whatever that they are a very low order of spirits, and scarcely ever those whom they personate. It is clear that Swedenborg never sent any such communications as these. To believe otherwise would be to believe that intelligent men in the other world lose their wits instead of increasing in wisdom. Doubtless this is permitted as a forcible and compelling offset to the tremendous and increasing materialism of the day. I can not conceive of any use in it to those who desire to be led by the Lord in freedom and reason. Not only Swedenborg declares the thing disorderly, but all experience coincides with his repeated warnings and emphasises the need of our keeping close to the Lord in his divine word. I say to you frankly that I do not feel warranted in putting this pamphlet before the society, for knowing as I do the seductive and tremendously persuasive power of this influence and realizing the evil in it, I should be doing violence to my sense of duty in bringing the matter to their notice. To those capable of better things it is a delusion and a snare. With kind personal feelings to you and all your family, and deploring your connection with this dreadful sphere, I remain sincerely yours in truth,

"John Goddard."

On November the 7th I repaired to Mrs. Green's, taking with me Mr. Goddard's letter, which I did not allow Mrs. Green to see, nor did I speak to her any thing in regard to its contents. I had also prepared a communication to Mr. Swedenborg, which I took along with me, in words as follows:

"To my exalted spirit friend, Emanuel Swedenborg: For conferring on me the honor of receiving your communications for the people who you seek to bless with the truth, I appreciate in the highest degree, and my only hope and wish is that I may be able to do this work in a proper and efficient way. The letter before you from the Rev. John Goddard, minister of the Church of the New Jerusalem here, in answer to my pamphlet containing your three first letters to me, is a sample of what may be expected from that class. I have had the opinion that the preachers of every denomination will be the very last to accept this most beautiful truth, and, therefore, I have concluded to send the pamphlet only to free, advanced minds, and to the individual members of the different churches of the New Jerusalem, if it receives your approval. With love and sincere affection, I am your willing and obedient servant,

"C. G. Helleberg."

Placing Goddard's letter with mine on the stand, the following communication came on the slate:

"In the adorable name of the Lord I salute you good morning. The course you have pursued in regard to my communications to you meets my hearty approval. In the future be governed by the directions of your immediate guides, in whom I have the utmost confidence, for they are constantly with you, and are more intimately related to your sphere, and know best how and what to direct. I am advised of the purport of the letter to you from our good brother, Mr. Goddard, and have lately visited him for the purpose of observing his surroundings and perceiving his mental operations. As the result, I believe him honest and nearer your platform than he is willing to make known. He certainly concedes enough in his letter to fortify your faith, and to satisfy those under his influence that modern spiritualism, so called, sprang from the great store house of the father's love, and is in his keeping. May the good brother become so illuminated as to reach the grander conclusion fully in consonance with the truth, that his religion emanated not from the Lord direct, but from the writer hereof under the spiritual instruction suited to that age, and that in lifting the veil between the two worlds of embodied and disembodied man, and permitting, yea compelling, the intercommunion between their denizens, the heavenly father has not made an assortment of evil only for you, for this would be malevolence under whatever pretext, but that all may, if they desire, hold intercourse with the terrestrial sphere. I have neither lost my wits nor retrograded in wisdom, but since I left the body I have lost much of my arrogance and pride, and am now more interested in imparting plain, simple truth, than in the construction of embellished sentences and high sounding and beautifully rounded periods. The humility taught by Jesus and others anterior to his day and since embodies a sublime law of the spiritual spheres, underlying all true progression, to which I cheerfully bow in reverential adoration. If my dear brother will only humble himself as a little child, forgetting for awhile his books, and casting aside the imperious demands of his system of belle-lettres, he will then from that truly spiritually elevated altitude begin to perceive and to drink in the beauties of spiritual truth and the glories of the Lord.

"Emanuel Swedenborg."

CHAPTER XIV.

COMMUNICATIONS FROM PRESIDENT GARFIELD, MADAM EHRENBORG, GOVERNOR J. D. WILLIAMS, PRESIDENT ABRAHAM LINCOLN, JUDGE EDMONDS.

Nov. 21. Among other things during this sitting with Mrs. Green I received the following:

"Good morning friends of truth. On passing out of the physical form and awakening to the consciousness of the perpetuity of my being, and a realization of my continued individuality, I was overwhelmed with the triumph of the spirit over the empire of crude matter, and as I gazed upon the worn, shattered and emaciated body, and in the presence of many kindred and other loving spirit friends, the first thought that occupied my mind was, is it possible that I have lived so long in the presence of this great truth and have known so little about it? Then followed a feeling of self-chiding, yea remorse, that I had neglected so many opportunities to learn that wisdom so much needed by the newly arisen spirit, and how much I had really missed by not acquiring knowledge of the spirit world, the future of the spirit, and the laws of spiritual government. Resulting from reflections like these came the impelling desire to return through whatever avenue I might find to speak to a fond mother, devoted wife, loving children, and sympathizing friends, to announce, if no more, that I not only still lived, but was fully conscious of and keenly alive to their grief and sorrow. But I would do more. Having passed safely and gloriously the ordeal of so-called death, and crossed the dreaded rubicon, I am now employing my best energies in learning the initial and rudimentary laws appertaining to spirit life and spirit growth, which I ought to have learned on earth, in the fervent hope and desire that I may be of service to my country and countrymen. If I have a friend who would hear and heed me, I would say to him as my best counsel, see to it that you learn more of the spiritual side of life while here in the body, that when you pass to the higher life your spirit may be accelerated in its onward march along the highways of progress in the heavenly spheres.

"J. A. Garfield."

At the seance the 7th of November, 1881, I placed a sealed letter, with no address on the envelope, on the stand, and no one in the body except myself knew the contents, as I had written it early in the morning at my home, on Mt. Auburn. I deem it best to give my letter and the answer to it in full, as it demonstrates beyond all possible controversy the ability of spirits to read and understand written matter effectually concealed from mortal view by being securely sealed up.

"To my dear exalted spirit friend, Madam Fredrika Ehrenborg: You always was on earth a valued friend of mine. Since your entrance into the spirit world I have been lead to appreciate more fully your good qualities of head and heart; and your kind spiritual ministrations to me I fear I can never repay. They have made me very happy indeed. You brought the highly exalted Swedenborg, and your angel husband to make God's truths clearer to us, and we know we can not return this loving kindness in any other way than in by trying to live up to them in our daily lives, and in making them known to others. During my whole life I have had so very few real friends outside of my family, but I now know that my good spirit friends have more than restored the loss of earthly friends, who I may have lamented. For a long time I have been thinking to send you a special offering of my sincere, heartfelt thanks, which I now do. Your sincere and humble earth friend,

"C. J. Helleberg."

The answer soon came in the following words on the insides of the double slate:

"To my highly respected earth friend, C. J. Helleberg: I know since my entrance upon a higher life more than before that you value my friendship to a very high degree, which I have tried with my spirit to reciprocate. You need not feel yourself under obligations to me or mine, for I take great pleasure in administering to your wants, and I am exceedingly happy to be able to do so, and that you appreciate we know. We are aware that our communications to you have made you and yours happy, and it rejoices us to know that we have been the instruments in doing good, and as you say, 'You can not return our loving kindness in any other way than by trying with all your might to live up to them in your daily lives, and in making them known to others.' That is just what your spirit friends wish you to do. You need not grieve for earthly friendship; those ties have soon to be broken, but have your thoughts on spirit life and friends? My noble husband and Mr. Swedenborg are here with us. Accept my heartfelt thanks for your good wishes toward me, and for your kind allusion to my noble companion. Love to your dear companion, and believe me ever your friend and guide. This is in answer to your sealed letters.

"Fredrika Ehrenborg."

The 23d of January, 1882, came the following from the former Governor of Indiana: "Good morning my dear friend in the cause of truth. I have been present at many of your sittings, and this morning I feel the power strong enough to write and give expressions to a few humble thoughts in regard to what I have done since my entrance to the spirit world. My battles here were to put down aristocracy and the expenses of our government. I fought hard for that. I did not believe in drinking ice tea at the expense of the government. I was satisfied with a good old fashion tea like my mother made, and a suit of blue jeans. I am still at work in our spiritual congress to that end. If there is not something done speedily our government of our forefathers is gone, and instead a stronger one, or monarchy. Capitalists gnawing at its vitals, and it must inevitably succumb. Spirit world is constantly at work to change the influence. We are coming to every channel we can to speak, and our prayers are that we may be heard and heeded. With my blessing on you both, I bid you good day.

"J. D. Williams."

"A. Lincoln, J. A. Garfield, O. P. Morton, A. P. Willard, Emanuel Swedenborg, Fredrika Ehrenborg, Madam Amalia de Frese, Polheim, Wilberforce and Otto Jacob Natt-och-Dag are present.

"Emil."

December 12th came the following:

"Kind friends: I am with you this morning to encourage you by the utterance of a few thoughts. The authority of the priesthood over the consciences and judgments of men is fast losing its hold, and creeds are in the course of ultimate extinction. The overthrow of the institution of slavery in the United States was precipitated by war, and I shudder to contemplate even the possibility that the final conflict between the prevalent creeds predicated on false theology, and succored by superstition on the one hand, and an enlightened rationalism, etc. on the other, may unhappily eventuate in bloody issues. Creeds are doomed to perish. God grant they may pass away without the costly sacrifice of blood. The pages of both sacred and profane history record crimes of the darkest and deepest magnitude enacted in the holy name of religion. In her fair name the soil of the earth has been crimsoned with the precious blood of martyrs, and the ghastly horrors of the inquisition have been feebly and imperfectly told. The real truth of those horrid deeds has been faithfully chronicled in the archives of the spirit world. Without malice, and in all charity, I speak of them to-day, but the truth must be boldly stated. The history of the Christian system of religion is, in part, a history of foul assassination, bloodshed and rapine, and all under the impious pretext of advancing the kingdom of heaven and magnifying the glory of the Lord. Not only have the brave souls who dared to lift voice or hand against the hideous monster of religious fanaticism and tyranny been sacrificed as heretics, but noble and queenly women—yea, innocent and unoffending children—have fallen victims to its merciless cruelty and gluttonous rapacity for greed and power. Religion and tyranny have marched hand in hand together along the highways of the past, and with the stake, the javelin, the executioner's ax, and every conceivable instrument of torture, have left behind them ruin, desolation and death as fitting and enduring monuments of their utter unrighteousness. Does this terrible history, so replete with evil, offer us evidences of Godlike excellence? Can such a religious system, founded in falsehood, fostered by superstition, nourished by the blood of innocence, and pre-eminently distinguished by so frightful a history, much longer command the tolerant and kindly consideration of the advanced intelligence of the world, or continue to inspire the conviction that it emanated from God, and has been sustained all these centuries by the fostering care of his goodness and love? In view of all this, is it surprising to any one that He who taketh cognizance of the minutest details of human conduct has commissioned his angels and the spirits who have escaped the environments and passed beyond the limitations of the flesh to return to those in mortal on the redemptive mission of demonstrating a continued life beyond the grave, and revolutionizing the religious thought, moral tendencies and spiritual conceptions of mankind. I repeat, creeds are doomed to perish, and this angel ministry, fraught with freedom, truth and righteousness, will erect her gorgeous temples over their buried ruins. Thanks be to God that I obeyed the majestic voices wafted from the spirit world, inducing, as they did, the liberation in our land of four millions of the enslaved children of chattel bondage. Enjoying the communion with spirits, and learning of them and their bright homes, the heritage of the father's love, I was, while yet inhabiting the tabernacle of clay, made glad and filled with superhuman joy, and in consequence was the recipient of strength and happiness in this glorious land of the spirit. Go ye, therefore, and do likewise. Good day.

"A. Lincoln."

CHAPTER XV.

NEW YEARS' GREETINGS FROM MANY OF MY DEAR SPIRIT FRIENDS AND NEAR RELATIVES.

The 29th of December, 1881, I received with many others the following communication:

"Good morning, my dear friends, for such I will call you, although I have never had the pleasure of seeing you in the body, but as magnetic attraction seems to be the topic, I will write a few lines to you. Some years ago I corresponded with this medium's husband, and I had the pleasure of calling her my pupil, because her mediumship was so much like that of mine and my daughter Laura. I took so much interest in her and her future success, and predicted that she would be a wonderful medium in time, and now I come as her teacher to congratulate her on her success and to give her words of cheer, and to tell her that she has only ascended half way up the ladder of fame as a spirit medium; and, also, that I have come to-day by magnetic attraction, and will be here often to aid her in her development. With my prayers for you both and for your success, I bid you good morning.

"Judge Edmonds."

The 2d of January, 1882, in the forenoon, came on the slate the following:

"Good morning, dear papa. We are all here with our happy New Year's greetings—Emil, Charles, Gustaf, Mary, Julia, Grandpa and Grandma Helleberg, Grandpa Natt-och-Dag, Swedenborg, Madam Ehrenborg, Madam de Frese, and a host of others. Dear Emil forgot me; I am last, but I hope not the least, in sending you a happy New Year's greeting. He says I am able to do that myself, and so I am, and happy to do so. Nothing affords me more real pleasure than to communicate to you. Wishing you many beautiful spirit communications this coming year, I bid you good day.

"Jennie."

After this came the following from a highly esteemed noble lady, who recently passed to the higher life, leaving an only daughter remaining in the form. Madam de Frese was distinguished in her native land—Sweden—for her literary tastes and labors and the purity of her character. It was a great surprise by reason of her having passed on so recently:

"Good morning, my dear friend. With the assistance of Mr. Swedenborg and our kind friend Madam Ehrenborg, and with the aid of this medium's very highly gifted and intelligent band, I am able to write a few more lines to those I love who are yet in the body." (At this moment I said to the medium, "It is my impression that this communication is from my friend, Amelia de Frese, and it may be a help to convince the New Church people in Sweden, and her daughter, of the spiritual truth and power.")

And then came:

"Yes, that is my object, to send them a New Year's greeting from my beautiful spirit home, and to tell my dear daughter that I am not far from her, but able to advise her and control affairs mundane, and that by impression. She will be directed in the right way, and although she does not imagine that I am with her, still it is a reality. Tell her to have no fear, she will be directed to do my will, and now that the dark pall is before her, and that to penetrate through it seems an impossibility, but 'ere long she will get glimpses of the summer land and of the loved ones gone before. Though the clouds may lower and thicken fast and the mutterings of the storm king is heard, fear not, mother is near to ward off danger. She will know my meaning. She is in mental trouble, the weight is almost overpowering. This will help to remove it somewhat, and what she longs for. She thinks, 'Oh, if mother could tell me what to do.' As a parting word, tell her that the sunshine of Spiritualism will scatter the clouds and mists that now surround her, and that she will be made doubly happy by its introduction into her troubled heart, and every pulsation of that member of the body will beat with joy. With the blessings of Swedenborg and Madam Ehrenborg, and with my heart full of love for her and highest regards for yourself and companion, and thanks for this privilege of communicating, I bid you adieu.

"Madam Amalia de Frese,
of Stockholm, Sweden."

January 9th I received the following from the same spirit:

"Thanks, my dear old friend, Mr. Helleberg, for sending the communication to my daughter. I will be there when she reads it, and make her feel my presence. I am your friend,

"Amalia de Frese."

CHAPTER XVI.

A PRAYER FROM MADAM EHRENBORG.

Jan. 26, 1882. And the following came on the slate, which I then copied word for word, and herewith reproduce *verbatim et literatum*.

"My dear old friend. According to promise I am here, and I will endeavor to write you a prayer:

"Oh, thou Infinite Spirit of Truth, soul of all things, we humbly approach Thee at this hour. We know our praises can not exalt Thee for Thou art already infinitely exalted. We know how vain are our adulations of Thee, and that we can not change or make Thee other than what Thou art, a being permeating all things, ever pure and changeless. We know Thou hast existed in all the past, and for Thee and Thine there is no ending in all the measureless immensity of future time. Thou art infinite and perfect in all Thy great attributes of love, wisdom, and power, the true and everlasting trinity. We know we serve Thee best when we seek and labor for the good of Thy children, whether they be in realms of spirit being or in mortal life. We feel the inspiration of Thy words—'Do good to all'—wafted to our anxious ears on every breeze, and we bow in reverence before the eternal words written on all the works of Thy mighty creation, 'Love one another even as I love all.' We look not for Thee in temples of human construction, or in buildings vainly dedicated to Thy worship, but we discover Thee in all that Thou hast brought into being by the creative energies of Thy almighty power. We hear Thy majestic voice in the mighty roar of old ocean and in the gentle murmurings of the brooklet. We hear Thy voice in the thunderings of the storm king and in the soft whisperings of the zephyrs. We behold Thee in the stately form of the oak and in the sweet blossoming and blooming flowers. Wherever we go, wherever we look, and in whatever we behold there Thou art ever present. Oh, Thou mighty master spirit of the universe, bless Thy children every-where. Strengthen Thy messengers, ministering spirits from the land immortal, to teach those still in the bonds of the flesh the sublime and eternal truths of immortality. May Thy children in mortal learn that wisdom which teaches righteous living, heroic dying, life-unending and eternal progression. Shower divine blessings on this aged brother who is seeking to know of Thee through Thy ministering angels. Strengthen his faith, increase his knowledge, cheer his heart, and as he nears the end of the journey of mortal life fill his soul with that joy that can only be bestowed by the spirits of dear ones who have passed to the better land. Bless, oh Father, this noble medium, a chosen instrument of the spirit world, through whom to transmit messages of love. Bless all such instruments. Encourage and invest with continually increasing powers this noble band of spirits, and enable them through their chosen and beloved medium to bless and cheer the hearts of many by the impartation of light divine, and may that light radiate through their souls as the sunbeams descending from the golden orb of day illuminates the physical world. Accept, oh Lord, from the fulness of our souls this our earnest prayer. Amen."

CHAPTER XVII.

GREETINGS FROM HORACE GREELEY, J. G. BENNETT, AND HENRY J. RAYMOND, TO F. B. PLIMPTON, ASSOCIATE EDITOR OF THE CINCINNATI "DAILY COMMERCIAL."

During the visit of the celebrated medium, Henry Slade, to Cincinnati, recently, a reporter of the Cincinnati "Daily Enquirer" visited him and secured a sitting, during which Mr. F. B. Plimpton, associate editor of the Cincinnati "Daily Commercial," by invitation was present. The day following, the "Enquirer" reporter, in speaking of the seance in the columns of his paper, referred to Mr. Plimpton in disparaging terms as being a believer in Spiritualism, etc. In the succeeding issue of the "Enquirer" Mr. Plimpton had published over his proper signature the following rejoinder:

DR. SLADE AND HIS "CONFEDERATE."

To the Editor of the Enquirer.

Your reporter makes much of my accidental meeting with him at the rooms of Dr. Slade. I had called on the doctor's general invitation (he being an entire stranger to me), not with the thought of witnessing any of the so-called manifestations, but to have a chat with him touching some points of his European experience.

In the course of our conversation he incidentally mentioned that he had an appointment with a press representative, and shortly afterward your reporter came in, and was introduced to me as "Mr. Culbertson." Having met the young gentleman on a recent social occasion, when he was introduced to me under his right name, his identity was not obscure to me, but it would have been the height of impoliteness on my part, an invited guest, to have interfered with any little plan he may have formed to entrap the magician. It is a trivial and common form of deception, and as Dr. Slade does not profess to be a mind-reader, it is as easy for a stranger to impose on him in that way as upon an ordinary person. So, as "Mr. Culbertson" your reporter remained from the beginning to the end of the sitting.

Why Dr. Slade changed his mind and allowed me to remain during the seance I do not know, and do not care to know. It seems, however, to have excited the suspicions of your acute reporter, who amusingly presents me to your readers in the light of a confidante of the doctor. This is too ridiculous to receive serious refutation. It was the sheerest accident that I was present at all.

Your reporter very fairly states the phenomena witnessed, except where his lively imagination charmingly interferes with strict accuracy, and tempts him to adorn his narrative with divers brass ornaments of his own invention. But he must pardon me if I decline to accept him as an expert at his own valuation, since by his own statement he stands condemned of practicing the only deception at all explicable, and then not telling the truth about it.

He is, however, entitled to his own conclusions, which must be very valuable, considering the time he has devoted to investigation. There is no accounting for the superior insight which a young man has into phenomena, that have baffled old heads after years of patient study. It may be remarked, however, that to denounce as trickery and fraud phenomena otherwise not easily explained is a ready way of ridding one's self of the whole business.

Though not giving much attention of late years to the subject, I am a Spiritualist, and not ashamed to own it. The time has passed when it is necessary to doff one's hat and apologize in this or any other intelligent community for being a Spiritualist. It is, at least, as creditable as to discourse without knowledge and condemn without investigation.

F. B. Plimpton.

On Thursday, February 2d, at Mrs. Green's, among other matter received came the following:

"Respected Sir: We are here this morning to ask you to go and see Mr. Plimpton, of the "Commercial," and say to him for us, that we not only thank but congratulate him for his recent bold and manly utterances in favor of truth. The time has arrived for those blessed with the knowledge presented by Spiritualism to bravely avow it, and we are glad that he has taken the initiative in the Queen City of the West. The time has truly passed when such avowal entails social ostracism or any kind of persecution. The banner of truth has been unfurled, and ye brave souls marshal the veteran hosts under it and onward to victory. You will find less obstruction than you think, for believers in this much-abused gospel of light are more numerous than you conceive. Besides you have myriad hosts of heaven at your backs. Falter not, move onward with firm and confident step. Be steadfast and true and bright laurels await you. The victory is not always to the strong, but to the active, the vigilant, and the brave. The army of Spiritualism has already swollen into huge proportions, and its ranks are being daily augmented. The decree has gone forth and the triumph will come. Truth shall arise for the eternal years of God are her's, and nothing can stay or retard the onward march to victory of the grand army of invisible hosts.

"Horace Greeley.
"J. G. Bennett, Sr.
"Henry J. Raymond."

CHAPTER XVIII.

COMMUNICATIONS FROM HORACE GREELEY, GOVERNOR O. P. MORTON, AND A. P. WILLARD.

On the 7th of April, among other things, I received the following:

"Unless some changes are made in the conduct of your government direful consequences are to be apprehended. Under the present mode of administration it is continually subjected to very heavy straining, and it can not much longer stand it. Many reforms are needed, and the requirements of patriotism demand that they be seriously considered and acted upon. Your civil service is entirely wrong, and can not be continued much longer without serious detriment to your form of government. The integrity and stability of your institutions are constantly menaced by it. You claim that you have an elective government. Is the claim true? Thousands of important public offices are not filled by the elective voice of the people. They are filled by appointment from purely partisan considerations—for partisan purposes and as a reward for party services and party zeal. Fitness and worthiness are secondary and minor considerations. Hence arise clamorings of party strife, and the engendering of the festering sore curses of corruption. The Presidential office had better be abolished than to continue it invested with such vast patronage in dispensing official appointments. There exists no valid reason why the people themselves should not select from their neighbors postmasters, revenue officers, etc., as well as state, county, and township officers. The Presidential office should either be dispensed with or its incumbent elected by a direct vote of the people without the intervention of the cumbersome and corrupting electoral machinery. The electing of men to elect other men to office is the dodging of a responsibility and the surrendering of a right of the people that can not be defended upon sound principles.

"Another danger confronts you menacingly and demands watchful attention. It is the startling aggregations of wealth among the few, and wrung from the sweat of labor. These immense accumulations find utilization in the creation of merciless monopolies which have already assumed gigantic and threatening proportions in the United States.

"Stock gambling is not a whit better in morals than any of the games of cards by which the unwary are fleeced out of their hard earnings. The participants and operators in the one are no better than in the other, and yet the one, under your Christian civilization is applauded while the other is denounced. How long yet will the people continue to be hoodwinked and handicapped by designing political tricksters. We have seen the star of hope, but now behold the star of promise rising in its refulgent splendor, and therefore we take heart.

"H. Greeley."

HON. O. P. MORTON.

On the 13th of April the following communication was received, purporting to come from the late United States Senator from Indiana, Oliver P. Morton, viz:

"Amid the rancor and jealousies of party strife I came in for a full share of abuse and vituperation. I was denounced most bitterly as an ambitious man, wholly unconscionable and indifferent as to the means employed in the accomplishment of party ends. Now, I frankly confess that I was not a saint in politics, nor always, politically speaking, perfectly orthodox. I am free to admit that I was so constituted that when I once believed a certain view to be sound and right I never hesitated to use all the appliances and machinery of party to secure its triumph. I was called a bold man in politics. I am proud of this, for it is in contradistinction to all that is sneaking. I aimed to always be right, and believed, in a certain qualified and honorable sense, that the ends justified the means. Those who are vociferating so loudly and screaming so painfully about bad and corrupt men, are generally traveling in the same boat, with the same sails spread to the breeze. In my mind and heart the country's good was always a paramount consideration, and I have as few regrets as most men who have devoted as long a period to public life. The man out of office feels himself called upon to denounce the man who is in, and affects to believe himself especially endowed with the requisite qualities to purify the public service, but when safely ensconced in the incumbency he too soon finds himself a Barkis, who "is willing." There are many good and true men engaged in public political life, but none perfect, and you would be as successful in ransacking *hades* for an angel of light in your efforts to find a perfect politician. Whatever is wrong and corrupt in your public service and political life will never be corrected and purified by the politicians alone. As well might you hope for a deadly eating cancer to eradicate itself, or the upas tree, with its deadly emanations, to give forth health-breeding and life-sustaining exhalations. The remedy rests alone and wholly with the great masses of the people. The prostitution of office to the debasing influences of bribery and corruption must be made odious by fixing austere penalties against the offender, and the prompt and indiscriminate enforcement of them. Misfeasance and malfeasance in public office ought to be considered an unpardonable crime, and the guilty dealt with accordingly. Let the people teach their officials the doctrine that a continuation of political existence depends wholly on fidelity to the public interests, and the honest, faithful and efficient administration of their official trusts. When there is willful dereliction of duty, or a failure by grossly reprehensible conduct to meet the just public expectations, not only relegate the offender to the walks of private life, but impose such punishment as shall be deemed adequate to the enormity of the crime, and will deter others from the commission of like offenses.

"O. P. Morton."

GOV. A. P. WILLARD.

May 19, 1882, I received the following from Ashbel P. Willard, who I learn was at one time Governor of the State of Indiana, viz.:

"Good morning, sir. I was, during my earth life, a politician, and, to a certain extent, a successful one, if success may be measured and determined by captivating the masses, and thereby securing elevation to office. I was in early life surrounded by poverty, and arose from humble conditions to the chief magistracy of the great commonwealth of Indiana. I was of the common people, always kept myself closely allied to them and their interests, and if you will excuse the egotism, always felt that I was near their hearts. I was called an orator, and probably to some extent this was true, for nature had favored me highly in that direction by organization, and I have occasion to be thankful that whatever gifts I may have possessed, they were aimed to be exercised for the promotion of the public good and the happiness and prosperity of the people. In youth I obtained a common education and taught school, and by teaching the young the rudiments of education I was enabled to study and observe the different tendencies and characteristics of mind. While engaged in this pursuit I discovered some properties of my own mind and some gifts of speech, which, in public utterance, subsequently distinguished me—not so much in the forum as on the "hustings" during periodical political excitements. I soon discovered that the power I was enabled to wield in political disputations was attracting the people to me, and their voices at the ballot-box soon called me into official position and consequent prominence.

"Whatever faults I may have had, it is a proud satisfaction for me to know that it was never charged that I ever betrayed either a private or public trust. But in my day things were quite different from what they are now. The politicians in my day were imbued with a different and a higher patriotic sense of obligation to the public interests and the general public weal. The great war of the rebellion seems to have poisoned the divine streams of patriotism, and the politicians of to-day seem to have drank too freely therefrom. You have passed through evil times, and they are still upon you.

"The best minds of the spirit world are hard at work seeking to purify the waters of political life. It must begin at the fountain head. The people, the great masses who constitute the fountain of all political power, must be awakened to a realization of the wretched condition into which they have permitted public affairs to drift. There must be a quickening of the public conscience and a revivifying of the patriotism of the early fathers of the republic. The sanctifying influences of the patriotism of the revolution must again permeate the hearts of the people. The politicians, always cunning and watchful of the tendencies and driftings of the public mind, will either fall in with the new order of things, or be forced to retire and subside from public notice. The great minds and patriotic hearts of Washington, Lafayette, Adams, Jefferson, Franklin, Hancock, Paine, Webster, Clay, Douglas, Lincoln, Garfield, and hosts of others, are coming from the skies, leaving for awhile the glorious pursuits and joys of spirit unfoldments to speak to the people, and to lead them away from the demoralizing and corrupting influences of the partisanship of the day into better channels and loftier patriotism.

"How shall the work of purifying the public service, restimulation of patriotism, and the placing of the waning fortunes of the country upon the high road of prosperity be done? *First.* What is needed to be done? *Second.* How shall it be done? These questions, so pregnant with mighty results, should engage your earnest and prayerful consideration. These matters may be discussed and presented to you, and I am glad that the means will be furnished to lay them before the people.

"If what I have said will be the means of arousing one patriotic citizen to the necessity of the governmental reformation now in contemplation by our spiritual congress, I shall feel then supremely happy that the little effort in writing these feeble lines was not in vain.

"I was known when in the form, and am still, as

"Ashbel P. Willard."

CHAPTER XIX.

COMMUNICATIONS FROM THE DRUNKARD, A MISER, WILLIAM GAILARD, WILLIAM LLOYD GARRISON, WILBERFORCE, TECUMSEH, A SUICIDE.

On May 25, 1882, came the following communication from a spirit, who declined to give his name, for reasons which he claimed to be prudential and personal to himself. It is here given in his own words:

"The band of spirits who have this medium in charge, together with other exalted ones and one who is co-operating with them temporarily, have not only allowed, but invited me, unworthy as I am, to come and tell my story. It is a short and terrible one, and in deep sorrow and humiliation I proceed to tell it.

"I was called, and justly so, a drunkard. By nature I was blessed with a strong and robust constitution, and I was, what is too often a curse, the child of wealthy parents. My father was rich, and this circumstance proved my ruin. I was nursed in the lap of luxury, never knew what it was to want, and consequently had no sympathy for those that suffered, or those immersed in the fierce struggles of poverty. I disdained to work with my hands for bread, and knew not the hardships and sorrows of the toiling millions. My brow was never moistened by the sweat of labor, and I grew up in the belief that the poor were intended and purposely created to serve the rich, and were deserving of naught but a bare scanty subsistence. My life of indolence and ease, my uninterrupted hours of leisure, produced their inevitable fruit in their accompaniments of vice and immorality. Idleness, as I now know, is the parent of vice, and riches too frequently constitute the propagating life germs of wickedness. It was sadly true in my unhappy case. Oh, fathers, mothers, heed my warning counsel: Train your children to labor—to work, work, work. Allow but few idle hours for dissipation and vice. Keep them away, if possible, from the club room, where intoxicating beverages are indulged in and made inviting by temptation, and where lascivious conversations only tend to stimulate and develop the lower passions and propensities of their natures. Wine, fair to look upon and with frequent imbibations exhilarating, contains within its alluring embrace a terrible lurking serpent whose venomous sting is fatal to all that is noble, grand, and holy. It strikes, figuratively speaking, its poisoned teeth into the very vitals of our being, and the effect follows us to the other life with its terrible retributive vengeance. Oh, pity the poor inebriate, and erect all possible barriers against the terrible ravages of the fell destroyer.

"The Drunkard."

A MISER.

April 24, 1882, came the following:

"I am permitted to come to you to-day to relate something of my history. There is a twofold purpose in my visit. I am told that this will greatly benefit me as a spirit still bound to my idol—gold—and that I may be instrumental in warning others to avoid my condition.

"I lived in the flesh more than three score years and ten, and when I laid down to die the only thing I regretted leaving was my gold and hoarded wealth. Oh, I thought, if I could only take it all with me how happy I would be. The world said I was a noble man, because being avaricious and greedy, I was successful in acquiring riches. My nobility of character was measured entirely by my ability to accumulate money and property. I want to publish it to the world that money, stocks, and landed estates, are poor capital to bank on in the spirit world. They will do here, and as the world goes, will make you respectable, your society and influence coveted and all that, but you need a different kind of capital on this side of life. Gold here has great purchasing power. It buys the luxuries of life, it even buys honor, virtue, and innocence, at a fearful sacrifice and cost to others, but its power, except its terrible evil following, ends with your life in the body. Nothing but good deeds, noble charities, and upright living pass current in the land of souls. I was a miserable, soulless miser, and my occupation and delight consisted in adding to my coffers, and in this endeavor I forgot and ignored conscience and every thing in the pathway of the pursuit of my idol.

"I belonged to a fashionable church, owned a pew, attended the services, and flattered myself that this was all that was needful to prepare my soul for happiness in the other world. No appeals of charity were ever strong enough to touch my sympathies or open my purse strings. The tears of the widow, the wails of the orphan, or the cries of the suffering, however piteous, never touched my heart or obtained from me a single penny. I stinted myself and family and contributed nothing towards the relief of want and suffering, for I was so completely enslaved by the accursed love of and passion for money. This is a humiliating confession to make, but it is, alas, for my happiness, too true. I tell you money has been my curse, and oh, how terribly have I suffered. Years upon years have rolled by, and I have only partially paid the penalty of my folly. No wonder the rich man wanted some one to go back and tell his brethren of his fate. I hope I may hereby be the humble instrument in warning others against the pitfall into which I have fallen. My gold came up before me here to greet my fond gaze, and when I would joyously reach out for it, behold it would elude my grasp, thus teaching me that it had no real existence except as the haunting specter of my unholy life struggle for its possession. The light of redemption now begins to beam upon me, flooding my soul with its bright rays of hope. I feel this will do me good, and I am very thankful for the opportunity. Let me be simply known as

"The Miser."

WILLIAM GAILARD.

William Gailard was an old personal friend, and the first one who called my attention to the subject of Spiritualism. He had been a Swedenborgian, and at times had officiated as a preacher in England before he came to the States. At a sitting with Mrs. Green, June 2, 1882, I was pleased to receive the following communication from him:

"My old friend, Mr. Helleberg. I know you have been waiting and wanting to hear from me, and I have been just as anxious to respond. Here in the spirit world we have order and system, and each one must bide his time. My time has come to speak a few words to you, and I assure you, my dear old friend, I seize the opportunity with pleasure I can not fully express.

"I remember that the new light of spiritual truth came to me first, and I was the humble instrument in the hands of higher intelligences to assist you in obtaining it. I was a medium for exalted spirits to lead you and others into the light, and that for a great and noble purpose, for way back to that time the plans were laid for the work in which you are now engaged so nobly and fearlessly. You are also, my dear friend, a medium, for it is true that all persons whom spirits can influence, however unconscious it may be to themselves, are mediums in the true sense of the word.

"You are helping others to grow and expand in spiritual knowledge, and you will be astonished when you come over to look back and see the work you have done, and to receive the plaudit, 'Well done, good and faithful servant.' I have been blessed beyond measure for the little I was enabled to do, but your reward will be greater than mine. Your opportunities were greater and you cheerfully yielded your energies, time, and means, to the work.

"If Spiritualists could only realize the treasures they are laying up for themselves by advancing the banner of truth, and the joys in consequence that await them on the golden shore, they would spare no pains or means and omit no effort in spreading the gospel of glad tidings. Oh, how I would exult with joy if the New Church people would see and preach this beautiful and blessed truth. They will yet get their eyes open, and step out of their little creed-bound narrowness, and stand upon the broad and heavenly platform of the Lord and this spiritual truth, for they are one and the same. Swedenborg will speak to them from the higher life, and I pray they may heed him. Your old friend,

"William Gailard."

WM. LLOYD GARRISON.

At the sitting June 9, 1882, came the following:

"For long years before the emancipation of the slaves I waged a fierce and bitter warfare against the institution of African slavery in the United States. The overthrow of that accursed institution became the absorbing and central idea of my soul from my early manhood. All other themes, questions, and subjects, I subordinated to that one dominant purpose of my life. When I had lived to see that institution swept out of existence, equal civil rights secured, and manhood suffrage conferred, irrespective of race, color, or previous condition of servitude, I felt a sweet heavenly calm rest upon my soul, accompanied by the consciousness that I had not lived in vain. I felt that my efforts, however feeble, had helped to forward to a glorious consummation that long eventful struggle, and that by aiding in pushing along the car of progress and freedom, the world had not suffered by my having lived in it. When the victory had been achieved I had advanced far 'into the vale of years,' and realized that my life forces were well nigh exhausted. They had been mainly expended in my life work as editor, lecturer, etc., in a warfare upon an unholy condition in which upward of four millions of human beings, with God-given souls, had been placed by sheer force and without their own consent. I saw and still see needed reforms that call aloud for help, willing souls, and ready hands. Reform in the currency, reform in the tariff, reform in the civil service, a complete overhauling and reconstruction of government, the overthrow of rum, and the enfranchisement of women. God will and is raising up noble souls for this noble work, and you may be assured that the spirit world is neither indifferent nor inactive. Spirit bands are forming every-where, instrumentalities are being chosen, and agencies are being arranged for the work. The millions of high and exalted souls of the higher life will, ere long, descend upon the children of earth with their inspiring and propelling influence, and a revolution in the realm of mind will be inaugurated that shall eventuate in the accomplishment of needed reforms. I shall be among the number with all my strength and soul.

"Wm. Lloyd Garrison."

WILBERFORCE.

July 7, 1882, at a sitting this day the following came:

"The main struggle of my life was to secure the liberation of the enslaved in the dominions under the authority and jurisdiction of the British government. I lived to witness the glorious success of my labors and to rejoice thereat and therein. I fought human slavery; I mean that slavery which is recognized by law—the right of one man to own another as a chattel, and to either transfer that ownership to another for a pecuniary or other consideration, or to transmit it as an inheritance. In doing so I had to combat wealth, prejudice, and biblical religion, for the bible recognizes this right. The struggle was long, eventful, and bitter, but victory finally crowned the effort. The civilized world concedes now the justness of my cause and the value to mankind of its success. And yet you are now fastening upon yourselves a slavery more appalling and degrading than African slavery ever was, or the slavery of the heathen and strangers of the olden time. (See Leviticus, 25th chapter, 44, 45 and 46th verses.)

"The slavery to which I refer now is the slavery of labor to capital. If I were back again in the body, with my present light on the subject, I would fight this accursed slavery more bitterly than I did that other species of slavery, which was bad enough, but infinitely less reprehensible than that which I am now discussing.

"No oppression is so utterly merciless and unconscionable as that of capital upon labor, and no other form of oppression can be so serious and hurtful in its consequences. Here we behold a mighty conflict between capital and labor. Capital making cruel and unreasonable exactions, seeking to obtain labor for an almost starvation pittance, while labor, unequal in the struggle, seeks to wrest from its adversary a decent and honorable requitement for its sweat. Capital triumphs and labor suffers. Let me tell you to-day, sir, and I would have the capitalists hear me, this contest will not always continue thus. Unless a spirit of justice and fair dealing shall speedily characterize the treatment of the poor toilers by their wealthy employers a mighty crash will come, an outburst of indignation in revolution that will render the bloody scenes of the past of trivial moment in comparison. The elements are generating, the storm clouds are surely gathering, and at a moment when least expected they will burst upon the country and the world in proportions only equaled by the fierceness of the conflict and its bloody issues. Let those whom it concerns beware. I beseech them, beware in time.

"Wilberforce."

TECUMSEH.

On the 4th day of August, 1882, between the hours of 9 and 11 A. M., came the following, which can not fail to be of interest to all who feel that our Indian policy has been either wrong or ineffective, and that the Indians have not been rightly treated. The eloquent simplicity of the communication can not fail to be observed:

"A large delegation of Indians are here and wish to be heard. We have concluded to let them speak. I will write what their leader says in as nearly his own words as possible.

"Nettie, *the Control.*"

"We come to speak to palefaces at Washington. Me talk for my people—the redfaces in the hunting-grounds in the Far West where the sun goes down. Poor redfaces, nearly all gone. Paleface kill many and drive them from their old and much loved hunting grounds. You tell them to go on reservation, and the big father at Washington take good care of them. They go. Big chief at big city send paleface agents to give them blankets, ponies, guns, and bread to eat. Paleface agent start big store in wigwam and cheat redface, and give him fire-water to make him mad and crazy. When my people see how they are cheated they get mad, and put on war paint and kill much. Big paleface chief say to blue-coat warriors, go and kill redface and make them come back, and let paleface agent swindle much more. Now this is all wrong, and if wrong, why not make wrong right. Redface only handful, paleface mighty—like the leaves on trees. If redface mighty and paleface weak, how then you like it? You then like redface be honest and not cheat, and do as big preach say about golden rule. Me no like you give my people fire-water or guns. Me much like better if you give red braves horses and plows, and build school-houses for little papooses. Teach them how to read and make big scratch (writings) and let them learn other papooses. Don't cheat. Put paleface clothes on redface, especially redface papooses, and learn them how to build big houses and how to raise big much to eat and sell. Then soon redface no more like hunting ground, but will love paleface and paleface ways. This much better than kill. Great Spirit no like paleface to kill redface or redface kill paleface. All die soon enough anyhow. Upper hunting grounds are full of redfaced spirits, and they all feel bad and sorry for redface in your land. Me no talk much more. Me sorry—me could cry. Poor redface few—soon all be gone. Be good to few left, and Great Spirit and redfaced spirits love you much. Spirit chiefs Ouray and Black Hawk and many more are here, and all plead for their people in lower hunting grounds. They all feel much bad. Good bye, chief and squaw. Me thank much for this big scratch.

"Tecumseh."

AN UNKNOWN SUICIDE.

August 28, 1882, the following was received, viz:

"I lived in the body thirty-five years and eight months. I went out by my own hand into the great beyond. I was a singularly constituted man, and a very unfortunate one. Self-love is said to be a great ruling passion, but I never loved myself, and of course could not be expected to love anybody else. My parents were in no way assimilated and lived very unhappily together. They quarreled and wrangled constantly, and this embodies my earliest recollection when a child, and it made an impression upon me from the influence of which I never recovered. They seemed to hate each other, and I was created and grew up under the same influence of hate, and hate accompanied by a feeling of vengeance and revenge became a predominating trait of my character. My parents both belonged to church, and I have seen them both shout in church (they were Methodists) and go home, quarrel and fight for hours afterwards. Father would get drunk and mother would eat opium. I tell you this disgusted me with religion, and I concluded it was all a farce. I believed death ended all, and that religion was either a delusion or downright hypocrisy. Besides I had a very delicate and feeble physical organization which made me more morose and sullen. Melancholy finally seized me as a victim, and in a moment of utter despondency I blew out my brains and ended life in the body. But I could not get away from life—death I found to be but the commencement of another life, and I had made the great blunder and committed the foul deed of taking my life into my own hands. Seventy-seven years have passed since, and the terrible shadow of the act of suicide still hovers over me and gives me pain and anguish. But thank God, I begin to climb up the mount of progression—but the summit is still far away. Oh, people of earth, I pray you become not the suicide. Wait with patience until nature's laws calls thee hence.

Remember the fate of the suicide is terrible and hard to overcome. And in my sad history fathers and mothers may learn an instructive and profitable lesson, for my father and mother have suffered more than I. Thanks for your goodness. Good bye.

"A Suicide."

CHAPTER XX.

COMMUNICATIONS FROM THOMAS PAINE,
MARGARET FULLER, AND THANKS OF SPIRITS.

Aug. 31, 1882. The following from the spirit of Thomas Paine, on capital punishment, was received:

"I am here to-day, sir, to say a few words in opposition to capital punishment. What is the argument in its favor? One citizen has taken the life of another citizen, and you say he has thereby forfeited his right to live. From whence do you get this doctrine? Does it belong to and is it a reflex of your boasted Christian civilization? The Mosaic law demanded an eye for an eye and a tooth for a tooth, but is this the doctrine of Jesus, the assumed founder of Christianity? If you think so, you certainly have not read him attentively, and it may be profitable to you in considering the subject to read the Sermon on the Mount, as recorded in the fifth chapter of Matthew, especially the thirty-eighth and thirty-ninth verses.

"You coolly and with the utmost deliberation usher these imperfectly developed souls out of one life into another, thereby ridding yourselves of human monsters and fiends by sending them to be cares, pests, and annoyances to the people of another world. And this you call Christian charity, benevolence, and fair dealing. But you say they can repent before they are shuffled off by the hangman, and thus be saved. If this be true, the best service you can render all villains and evil disposed persons is to hang them as the surest means of saving their souls in heaven, for if they are permitted to live and die natural deaths the chances are that they will never repent, and all consequently go to hell. But this is a subterfuge. It is the unholy spirit of revenge that actuates you, and you consider not the victim's good. Certainly heaven is not yearning for these cutthroats and outlaws, and hell, according to orthodoxy, is already crowded and overpopulated. One man, either through ungovernable passion or malice prepense, takes the life of another. Now, he generally has some real or imaginary grievance, but without even this excuse your courts take the other life, just as if one wrong justified another. Your plea that protection to society demands this course is untenable. Is it true that no adequate protection can be afforded except by judicial murder? Would not the confinement of the culprit subserve the same purpose, with the additional humane advantage of allowing the opportunity to reform and become better, and best of all, to let the voice of God, through natural law, call him from time to eternity.

"Christians can not rise up to the sublime altitude of adopting, in practical life, the ennobling teachings of the Nazarene including love and forgiveness, as long as they believe the God of their worship to be a vindictive and passionate being full of spleen and vengeance. To believe in such a God naturally inspires the effort to imitate his characteristics, and hence they become spiteful and vengeful, and in favor of taking human life on the scaffold, because a badly organized mortal in a fit of rage or in the pursuit of revenge for, perhaps, an imaginary wrong done him, slays his neighbor. The killing of one man by another is no worse than judicial murder, and both are relics of barbarism and a past heathen age, and you ought to have done with them. To-morrow, Margaret Fuller on prayer.

"Thomas Paine."

MARGARET FULLER.

Sept. 1, 1882, came the following writing from the spirit of Margaret Fuller:

"True prayer is the yearning of the soul for something it feels the need of. It need not be expressed in silent words or oral declamation. Every aspiration is in the true sense a prayer. Every aspiration, though silent, has its potencies, reaches out and attracts its kindred spiritual affinities. If your soul-yearnings and aspirations are of a sordid and purely earthly nature, they affect and attract corresponding influences in the invisible realm of being, permeate your soul and limit it to that sphere. If, on the other hand, your aspirations pertain to the realm of the lofty and beautiful, you render yourself thereby receptive to the grand and ennobling influences of the pure and heavenly. If you pray for riches in a worldly sense you prepare the mental, moral, and spiritual conditions to attract the spirit misers and the selfish. If you pray for spiritual illumination and aspire to moral excellence, you bring to your sphere and aid the noble and unselfish children of the more exalted spiritual spheres. If you meditate a wrong deed or action you will be successful in drawing to your assistance those unfortunates of the spirit world who have not outgrown the tendencies, inclinations, and imperfections, of their earthly careers and conditions. Hence the very great importance of being mindful for what you pray. The spiritual influences that you attract and which thereby become associated with you, exert a powerful influence in directing your footsteps, molding your actions, and in the construction of your spiritual temple in the new life just before you. Would you desire the companionship of spirit paupers and spirit tramps, become one yourself, and you may depend on success. Would you prefer rather to be attended by good and noble spirit and spiritual influences, aspire to be good and noble yourself, and your success is assured. Of one thing be enlightened, your spirit attendants during your mortal journey will be no worse than you are yourself. It is yourself that prepares the conditions and not they. If your actions are upright, your aspirations noble, and your thoughts elevated toward the divine, you thereby exert a positive repellant power that no evil can overcome, and in such a generated atmosphere an evil influence can no more dwell than oil can mix with water. Bear this great law in mind, and take advantage of it and you are safe and all will be well. Heed it not in conduct and thought and it will rebound upon you with damaging effect.

"Hesitate not to invite undeveloped spirits to your seances if your purpose be to benefit them. For such a motive on your part will draw around you the encircling influences of angels and the divine protecting love, and no harm can befall you, but much good to the poor spiritual wanderers in spiritual darkness. They must be lifted up, and you can be of great service as auxiliaries to the advanced spirits who labor for their redemption. By such a course you are praying such prayers as will bring upon you blessings from the angelic spheres

"Margaret Fuller."

At the same sitting came the following closing remarks by the medium's immediate control:

"I am requested to state that with this ends the present book, and to express to you, Mr. Helleberg, the thanks of the spirits who have communicated for your attentiveness, painstaking, and honest purposes. The band of the medium have done all they could to assist them and from them have received benedictions. Besides it has been a labor of love on our part to be, in any sense, assistants to so many exalted spirits.

"We also thank you for your gentlemanly deportment towards our medium, and for the earnest and honest interest you take in her welfare. I speak for the entire band.

"Nettie, *the Control.*"

CHAPTER XXI.

MRS. GREEN'S MEDIAL HISTORY.

The following is a partial history of the development and mediumistic experiences of Mrs. Lizzie S. Green, the medium chosen by the spirits in transmitting the matter contained in this volume:

She was born in Jefferson county, Kentucky, on the second day of December, 1844, and consequently at this writing is in her thirty-eighth year.

The following narrative of her mediumship was written by her husband, dictated by herself, and when written out was pronounced by her to be correct, and she adopts it her own. It is believed that this briefly recited history can not fail to be interesting to the general reader, since it contains matter and experiences not only absorbingly interesting but truly wonderful, and evidences the existence of a power that all thoughtful and candid persons will agree is worthy of investigation.

Those who have enjoyed Mrs. Green's acquaintance socially for years invariably speak of her as a truly honest woman, faithful wife, loving mother, steadfast friend, in intellectual capacity far above and beyond her educational advantages, and as possessed of many other sterling qualities of heart. Those who have come in contact with her in the exercise of her medial gifts can not fail to have been impressed with her frankness, simplicity of character, and the unquestionable honesty of her nature.

Lizzie Shirley Green

This tribute to her integrity and moral worth is given because well merited, and by one who not desiring notoriety and fame wishes simply to be known as

A Friend.

NARRATIVE OF HER MEDIUMSHIP.

"My conscious mediumship began in the fall of 1868. It commenced by the opening of my spiritual vision, enabling me to see spirits, scenes, landscapes, etc., in their spirit world. When in the proper state or condition of passivity I have been permitted to behold innumerable throngs of spirits, and at times to hear their voices. The phase of clairaudience added to my clairvoyance I prized highly, and sorely regret that shortly afterwards a fit of sickness deprived me of the gift of hearing spirit voices, and for a time seriously retarded my other mediumistic development. I am happy to be able to state, however, that with my gradual restoration to health my clairvoyant perceptions began to increase in power and beauty, and now the voices of the arisen dear ones again greet my anxious and ever attentive ears.

"I desire to state in this connection that in all my intercourse with spirits they have never deceived me in a single isolated instance. They have always been truthful and straightforward in their statements and dealings with me.

"In the earlier stages of my mediumship and still sometimes I was frequently controlled to personate the peculiar and characteristic idiosyncracies of spirits during earth life, and to delineate their sickness and death. Sometimes I would be rendered entirely unconscious and at other times only partially so. I shall never forget one memorable occasion of complete unconsciousness and the occurrence during it as related subsequently by eye witnesses. An old lady was present in the circle who I had never met before, and of whose history I had no means of obtaining the slightest knowledge. At the time I was wholly ignorant as to whether she had ever been a mother or the maternal head of a family, until I saw and described minutely a spirit standing by her side, who she readily recognized as her deceased son. 'What was the cause of his death?' she eagerly inquired. Almost instantly my consciousness was suspended, preceded by a violent tremulous motion all over my frame. I fell to the floor in a violent fit, and so terrible was it, and so true to nature in all its terrible details that no little alarm was manifested by the various members of the circle. It thoroughly demoralized and threw them into consternation. I need only add that old Mother Thompson (for that was her name) has never since doubted the return of the spirit of her son George, for the poor man had not only suffered a quarter of a century from that appalling affliction, epileptic fits, but actually died in one. I soon recovered my normal condition and received the apology from the spirit for having used me so roughly, stating that his extreme anxiety to convince his beloved mother of his presence induced him to disregard delicacy and to overcome all obstacles in the way of the accomplishment of his purpose.

"A little girl came to me on a certain occasion and said to me, 'Please go and see my mother and tell her I am not dead.' 'Where does your mother live?' I inquired. After giving me the necessary directions where and how to find her, I said: 'But your mother is a stranger to me, and perhaps if I go to her on an errand of that kind she will drive me from her door.' 'No she won't,' interposed the little pleader, 'she will be glad to learn that I am not under the cold ground but alive.' I marshaled the courage to go, yet I greatly feared the result. I was met at the door by the one I desired to see, and without giving sufficient time to explain the object of my call, I was cordially welcomed indoors. After being seated, and after the usual courtesies had passed, I opened the subject by saying, 'You have a little girl that has gone to the other world?' 'Yes,' said she, falling into tears, 'she was a dear, darling child, and I have had no rest since she left me. She was the idol of my heart, and it seems that I can never become reconciled to her death. Really, at times, I can scarcely realize that she is dead.' Here a pause ensued, and her grief was so intense that the waters of sympathetic sorrow involuntarily flowed down my own cheeks. Rallying, however, as quickly as I could, I said: 'My good woman, your Mary is not dead. She stands there by your side and wants me to say to you, 'Mother, I am not dead; do not weep for me, for I am still with you.' 'How! What does this mean?' exclaimed the mother in apparent bewilderment, 'I saw her poor little precious body consigned to the cold and cheerless grave.' 'Yes,' I interrupted, 'but her spirit—the immortal and only valuable part of herself— was not buried beneath the ground. Hold, she wishes me to describe her, and further, to prove her identity. She is a bright, blue-eyed girl of eleven or twelve summers, light auburn hair naturally inclined to curl, and falls in beautiful ringlets around her neck, forehead of the Grecian mold, face even and rounded, with a mark resembling a raspberry under her right eye, and she died from scarlatina.' 'Why, did you know Mary when she was living?' was immediately asked. I assured her I did not. 'Does the description fit her?' I inquired. 'Perfectly,' was the reply; 'who told you about her,' she added. I answered: 'My good woman, believe me, until to-day I did not know you were in existence. The facts I have stated to you I obtained from your Mary without the slightest knowledge of either your or her history.' After further conversation on the subject, and after describing other spirits, whom she readily recognized, the interview terminated, with a pressing invitation to return, and the assurances that she had derived from my visit inexpressible joy and happiness. In a few days thereafter I was unexpectedly called away from St. Louis and have never returned. Letters from friends who were cognizant of the circumstance as related by herself, inform me that Mrs. Collins is happy in the knowledge of spiritualism, has become reconciled to the temporary absence as to physical form of her child, and sends me her benedictions.

"In 1869 while holding a circle at Aurora, Ind., composed of a few intimate friends and neighbors, a gentleman—a stranger to all of us—applied for admission, stating that he had been left by the east bound train, and not being able to resume his journey until the following morning, and hearing of my mediumship, he desired, if agreeable, to have a sitting, or be allowed to join the circle for that occasion. My husband cordially assented. Our stranger friend had been seated but a short time when I saw a spirit forming by his side. I watched the process, and to my utter astonishment, which I at once made known, the spirit had a rope around his neck and presented a frightful appearance. I observed, 'I see a spirit with a rope around his neck, with tongue protruding,' etc. 'Describe him, madam, if you please,' spoke the stranger. I did so; the spirit for the purpose changing his appearance to that of his natural condition. The stranger became very much excited, arose, seized his hat, and nervously remarked, 'This is a great test to me. Several years ago I was sheriff of an interior county in Indiana, and that man, Jim Roberts, was sentenced to be hanged for the murder of his father-in-law, and I am the one who executed the sentence of the court.' When in the act of taking his departure, he suddenly turned around, and plaintively inquired: 'Has Jim got any thing against me? I only did my duty as an officer of the law.' On being assured that no ill feeling was entertained by the spirit against him, but that he appeared as he did more for the purpose of a test than any thing else, he took his departure. I have never seen him since. He gave me, however, considerable notoriety in the community by relating his wonderful experience with a spiritual medium, and advised every one to shun mediums unless they were prepared and willing to have every thing connected with their past lives revealed and made known. Perhaps this abused spiritualism may yet become the instrumentality of compelling people to walk uprightly in their dealings with their fellowmen.

"These are a few among hundreds of such instances that I might relate, but the space allotted will not permit. I wish now briefly to refer to another phase of my mediumship. At various intervals I have had prophetic warning, and prophetic revelations have also been given me. I have also had what might be appropriately termed panoramic visions of past events of those both in and out of the body, and of events to transpire in the future of earth life. These visions, especially those prognostic of the future, have been truly wonderful. It is an oft quoted saying that 'coming events cast their shadows before,' and there remains no doubt in my mind but what spirits—whether all, I am not prepared to say—can sufficiently forecast the future as to reveal events and actions concealed from mortal discernment in the bosom of coming time. Let me mention a few instances in my own experience as evidence of the existence of this power.

"In 1869, myself and husband were holding a seance alone, at Aurora, Ind. We were living in the lower part of the city, near the river bank. Aurora is situated on the banks of the Ohio river, twenty-five miles below Cincinnati, Ohio. A little above the center of the city fronting the river a small stream, called Hogan creek, empties into the Ohio. Three or four hundred yards above the junction of the two streams and on the banks of the aforementioned creek, is located the mammoth distillery, owned by Messrs. T. & J. W. Gaff & Co. It has been consumed three times by fire and as often rebuilt. At the time of which I am speaking, we put blankets up to the windows in the room to be used for our dark circle, and by this means effectually excluded all external light. After extinguishing our lamp light, we sat patiently, awaiting manifestations. In the course of a half hour I saw and said, 'I see a large brick building on fire. The light from its ascending flames is flooding the river in front of the city. There, I see a poor man burning up in the fire. I see its majestic walls crumbling to pieces and falling into a huge mass of ruins.' At this juncture, we heard out doors the cry of fire! fire! and soon the bells of the quiet little city began to announce to its citizens that the insatiate fire-fiend was engaged in his terrible work of devastation and ruin. We hastened to the door only to behold, true to the vision previously given, the bosom of the river as brilliantly lighted up as though illuminated by the rays of the sun at his meridian height. T. & J. W. Gaff & Co.'s distillery was on fire and burned to ruins, and another concomitant of the vision was too sadly verified—a man was literally burned to ashes.

"Soon after this occurrence, a very dear lady friend called to see me. She contemplated a trip to Indianapolis, and intended to start on the morrow train. I said to her, 'Do not start to-morrow. Defer it until the succeeding day. I see an accident on the road, and I see written in the air these words, "Within twenty-four hours."' I prevailed on her to postpone the trip in accordance with the warning of the vision. She had no occasion to regret it for the train on which she intended to be a passenger jumped the track before it reached its destination, and while no one was very seriously injured, yet it might have been otherwise had my friend been on board. She might not have escaped so luckily.

"The shocking casualty of the collision between the United States mail steamers America and the United States, on the Ohio river, between Cincinnati and Louisville, will be well remembered, especially by the people along the line of that route. The night of the painful occurrence I was a member of a circle held at the residence of Mr. Lewis Shirley, of Jeffersonville, Ind. I saw the collision, the boats on fire, etc., at an hour antedating by several hours the time when the unfortunate event transpired. So thoroughly was I convinced that the verification of the vision was close at hand that I prevailed on a son of Mr. Shirley to meet the carrier-boy at the ferry landing early the following morning to procure a copy of a Louisville daily paper. When the boy returned with the paper I was not surprised to find in its columns an account of the disaster, which I had plainly and vividly seen a number of hours prior to its actual occurrence.

"On another occasion I saw a fire raging. I saw it was a two-story brick house. I saw men rolling barrels out of the burning structure, and from the rapidity of their movements and the ease and facility with which the barrels seemed to be handled and propelled along, I concluded they were empty and so expressed myself. My husband inquired, 'Where is the fire at?' I placed myself in as passive a state as possible, but could get no answer. The questions were then asked: 'Is it Louisville?' 'No.' 'Is it

Jeffersonville?' 'No.' 'New Albany?' 'No.' 'Indianapolis?' 'Yes.' These answers respectively I saw written in the air or what appeared so to me. On that night, as we learned by the papers subsequently, a large barrel factory at Indianapolis was destroyed by fire.

"I will now relate one of a more startling nature and of more recent occurrence. The ill-fated steamer Pat Rogers was at the time of her destruction in the mail line service, and plied between Cincinnati, Ohio, and Louisville, Kentucky. She left port Louisville for Cincinnati at 2 P. M. At 4 o'clock, same afternoon, and two hours after her departure from Louisville, and nine or ten hours before the terrible casualty, I saw written in the air, 'Steamboat disaster to-night.' My husband remarked: 'See if you can not get the name of the boat.' Presently I saw plainly the name Pat Rogers, which was immediately followed by presenting the whole vision, the conflagration, and passengers struggling for life amid the angry and turbulent waves.

"I might narrate many more instances of this kind that belong to my individual experience, and volumes might be written if similar experiences of others should be included.

"I come now to speak of my present powers and their development. When my husband had entered upon his second term as Mayor of the city of Aurora, he built us a home in a high altitude on a hillside overlooking the beautiful city in the valley below. Here in the purer atmosphere with quiet surroundings were my present powers brought forth by a noble and trusty band of spirits whom I shall never cease to love for their fidelity to me and to truth, and for their ability and unceasing and intelligent efforts to advance the great and blessed cause of spiritualism. My dear spirit sister, Alice Vernette Winesburgh *nee* Shirley, who, in her day, was a marvelous physical medium, has been and still is the active controlling spirit of my band, with others great and good, who sustain and aid her. She always signs her name simply

Nettie, by which she was called and known in earth life. She has clung to me with the true devotion of a sister, and has sustained herself in the position assigned her by the band with signal fidelity and ability. I shall speak more of this band toward the close.

"In obedience to the request of the spirits we formed a circle for development, and found two gentlemen and their wives who were sufficiently liberal, and who had natural tendencies toward a belief in spiritualism. They agreed and we met twice each week, and it was not long before we discovered that power for physical manifestations was being developed. We sat in the dark around an ordinary plain stand, on which was placed a slate and pencil, a small bell, and a paper horn. We also would place on it a goblet filled with water. The manifestations began by the stand moving around and tipping. This phenomenon soon occurred in the light, and by means of it we at first were directed and instructed, using the alphabet in spelling out words. We met regularly and sat patiently. For a few months the development was slow but surely indicated progress, and the invisible operators continually exhorted us to patience, promising certain results from time to time, which they invariably performed. They stated to us what may not be generally known, namely, that all developments with a view to permanence are slow, advancing cautiously, step by step, leaving nothing neglected or uncared for. Besides the health and well being of the medium should be carefully guarded and too oft by hurrying forward the development ruinous consequences resulted to the instrument and the success of the mediumship. We soon noted the fact that we were in the hands of careful, prudent, and able spirits, and we therefore implicitly obeyed their directions, and have never since had any occasion to regret it. Finally the bell began to ring, and the various members of the circle were touched by materialized spirit hands. Also, names and words were written on the slate and occasionally materialized locks of hair would be found on the stand upon closing the seance, which, in a few hours, would wholly dematerialize. This indicated materialization of spirit forms and was so announced to us. The next step was whispering to us through the paper trumpet, and by that means they were now enabled to give directions. After the lapse of about twelve months we were directed to procure a curtain for materialization, which we accordingly did, but before this the manifestations in the dark had become simply remarkable, not to say extraordinary. On putting up the curtain and taking my position behind it, several sittings passed without any appreciable result, until finally faces were discovered protruding from behind and above the curtain, two or three at a time, and after this it was not long until full form materializations were obtained. Upon the expiration of my husband's term of office, the band insisted that we should move to Cincinnati, if only for a year, assigning as the important reason, that they would be enabled there to collect and appropriate new elements necessary in the completion of the development. We had by this time learned that the wisest thing was to obey, and consequently in July, 1881, we moved to the Queen City. Soon after we got there the band concluded to abandon for the time being any further attempt to perfect the phase of materialization and demanded a tin trumpet, which was made according to their directions. In length, thirty-eight inches; at large end, four and one-half inches in diameter, and at the small opening one-half inch; and we commenced holding trumpet seances with amazing and astonishing results. Hundreds of the best citizens of Cincinnati can testify to the wonders of the trumpet circle in my presence. One seance written up by Judge A. G. W. Carter, of Cincinnati, I here insert as illustrating partially only the magnitude of this power. It appeared in that excellent paper, *Mind and Matter*, of Philadelphia:

"My wife and myself, by invitation, were present on Thursday night, January 26th, at a seance given to a select circle of ladies and gentlemen by Mr. and Mrs. Green, at No. 309 Longworth street, this city, where Mrs. Green daily and nightly sits, giving private seances through her mediumship to any person or persons who desire to converse with the spirits, or see manifestations, and learn about the spirit world. There were about twelve persons, ladies and gentlemen, present, and being seated according to the direction of the spirits, a dark circle for spirit manifestations was held, and with extraordinary success. There was a large trumpet or horn standing beside the table, and a small music box and a guitar and a tambourine on the table.

"It was not long before the music box began its music, as well as the guitar and tambourine, and they all floated through the air, around the circle, and above our heads, and sometimes touching each one of the circle, as they were giving forth their music. Singing was indulged in by the members of the circle, and during the songs, the long horn or trumpet moved from its place, and went about the circle, through the air; and through it, or inside of it, different spirits accompanied the singing with their voices; sometimes so loudly as to take the full burden of the songs upon themselves. Then, when there was a cessation of singing, by means of the trumpet the spirits would freely converse with us—some in whispers, and others in sonorous voices, so that the whole company could readily hear and easily distinguish what was said.

"At one time one of the company, a Swede, Mr. Helleberg, sang a Swedish song, accompanying himself on the guitar; and in singing and playing this song in his native and, to us, foreign language, he was accompanied by a loud female voice, singing in his language, through this same horn. Mr. Helleberg then sang a Swedish love song, and was again, in perfect soprano harmony, accompanied by the female spirit voice.

"These demonstrations I thought were most remarkable, as I had never seen nor heard the like before, and they fairly attested the great mediumistic ability of Mrs. Green. At this time, and indeed during the whole seance, Mrs. Green was in a profound trance at the table, and kept so by a rough and gruff Indian spirit, who called himself 'Chip,' and occasionally spoke to us in a rough and gruff way about his 'medy,' and the power he had to invoke and exercise in keeping her in the profound trance condition. Ever and anon, also, a smart, witty and talkative Indian maiden, who called herself 'Winnie,' by the permission and condescension of 'Chip,' would take possession of the medium, and talk most freely and interestingly to each and all of the members of the circle.

"And, by the way, I must relate this peculiar and remarkable fact, the only time of its occurrence in all my long experience with the spirits. There was in the circle another trance medium, Mrs. Taylor, who was put into the trance condition very easily and readily. Well, this spirit 'Winnie' would exchange from Mrs. Green to Mrs. Taylor every once in a while, talking through each medium with equal facility, and to the great delight and edification of the members of the circle. This was indeed something remarkable, and I ventured to inquire of the spirit 'Winnie' if this was a common occurrence. She replied, through one of the mediums, that it was so uncommon that she never knew of it occurring at a circle sitting before; that spirits always had their own medium, and it was very seldom that they would or could talk through more than one chosen medium, and especially at the same sitting of a circle, as was the case with us.

"To narrate all that occurred at this remarkable seance would fill many printed columns. Sufficient for the present to say, that we had all sorts of manifestations from the spirits through the gifted medium, Mrs. Green, for the long period of three full hours, and yet the medium or the spirits were not at all exhausted, and apparently not even fatigued. The manifestations, it seems to me, were quite equal to any I ever witnessed from Maud Lord, or any of the best mediums, and convinced me beyond all manner of doubt, that the gifted Mrs. Lizzie S. Green is destined to take a prominent and important stand in the glorious domain of mediumship. Angels bless and take care of her in all her ways.

"A. G. W. C."

"In the meantime, the independent slate writing progressed wonderfully, and now constitutes one of my best and most highly cherished phases. They write now with the utmost facility with their own materialized hands, and, strange as it may seem, they have actually written without the presence of any visible pencil at all. They have written long messages on the inner surfaces of double slates, the parties holding on to them at the time the messages were being written. They have done this for me in the presence of C. G. Helleberg, John Winterburn and William Layton, and others, honorable people of Cincinnati, who will take great pleasure in certifying to the same. I do not refer to these truly marvelous things in a spirit of egotism or self-boasting, for I am entitled to no credit except in so far as I may have, by prudent conduct, honest living and carefulness, assisted in securing the proper conditions for the invisible intelligences—I mean invisible to mortal eyes only. While I naturally feel proud of these noble gifts, I have learned to be humble with them, as my spirit guides have so often admonished me to be. And I feel like using them for the benefit of humanity and the upbuilding of truth.

"My clairvoyance was an early and permanent development and still remains with me, the other development not seeming to materially interfere with it.

"I have had with me for many years two Indian spirits, from whose association I have derived great pleasure; and I have ever found them true, faithful and honest. The male Indian has never given me his full and proper name, telling me that it was ugly. He was of the Chippewa tribe, and has always been known as 'Chip.' Chip abhors fire-water and tobacco, and every thing immoral, and in very many respects widely differs from the leading characteristics of his people. The Indian maiden, whom we call Winnie, came to me in 1868, and gave her name as Winniepesaga, and said while quite young she was drowned in a stream of water in the Far West. She is sprightly, quite talkative, exceedingly smart and interesting in conversation. Naturally gifted with clairvoyant powers and prophetic abilities, she has given very many remarkable tests, and by reason of her equability of temper, general good disposition and real cleverness in colloquial gifts, she is generally well liked by all who have come in contact with her spirit ministrations. She has controlled me for years, does yet, and her influence is sweet, soothing and strengthening. Captain Oliver C. Curry died at Jeffersonville, Ind., in 1874, and was a lawyer by profession, and was for a long time city attorney of that city. He was a cousin of mine, and has belonged to the band for two years, and has been exceedingly active, especially in the trumpet seances. By his suavity, intelligence and witty sayings, he has made himself quite a favorite with many. Assisting in the development, I have had with me several spirits familiar with the laws of science, including a distinguished French scientist, our own Franklin and Professor Mapes. They seem to have only been engaged with the band temporarily in aiding the advancement of the development. They have my sincere thanks and profound gratitude. I come now to speak of another spirit, although of an humble name, yet a grand and highly progressed one, who has been my leading counsellor, adviser and friend. In 1868, I laid away the lifeless form of a dear little boy, and in my unutterable grief this noble spirit first appeared to me and gave me words of consolation. He has been with me ever since. He passed out of the form in the State of Georgia at the early age of thirty-three and had been at the time he came to me upwards of fifty years in spirit life. He always inspires me as being the very embodiment of purity itself, and his whole ambition seems to be to do good. This spirit also possesses wonderful prophetic power, and communicates with me only in case of an exigency, when I am in trouble, or otherwise need the sustaining and guiding power of the angel world. He gives me his name as Henry Teaney, and no Christian ever worshiped the gentle Nazarene with more devotion than I do my friend and guide, Henry Teaney. He is pure, noble and godlike, loves the right, hates the wrong, and never condescends to any thing little, hateful, or mean.

"Here I close after again returning thanks from the inmost recesses of my heart to my honored and noble band of spirits engaged with and through me in the great work of advancing the kingdom of God in the dissemination of truths vouchsafed to the children of earth through spirit communion."

CHAPTER XXII.

A VISIT TO SPLIT ROCK, KENTUCKY—CHRISTMAS GREETINGS FROM IDA TO HER PARENTS—ANNIE WINTERBURN TO HER BROTHER JOHN WINTERBURN, AND HIS TESTIMONY AND HER FAREWELL TO THE MEDIUM, MRS. GREEN.

Mrs. Green's home proper, is at Aurora, Dearborn county, Indiana. Aurora is a beautiful and enterprising little city of five or six thousand inhabitants, and is located on the western bank of the Ohio river, twenty-five miles or thereabouts below Cincinnati, Ohio. It can be reached from Cincinnati in less than an hour's ride over the Ohio and Mississippi railroad, which passes through it. While her husband pursues the legal profession at Aurora, Mrs. G., in obedience to the wishes of her spirit guides and attendants, devotes her time and medial gifts at Cincinnati from Monday until Saturday of each week, returning to her companion and daughter each Saturday, and remaining with them over the Sabbath. This statement is deemed proper in view of and as prefatory to what I am about to relate as occurring recently, and which can not fail to be estimated as a truly remarkable spirit manifestation.

By the invitation of Mr. Green, Mr. Edwin Stebbins, of Cincinnati, and myself accompanied Mrs. Green to her home at Aurora on Saturday, August the 5th, for the purpose of joining a small party of excursionists on the day following to the celebrated Split Rock, some three miles down the river from Aurora, on the Kentucky side of the Ohio. Our host had chartered a small propeller steamboat known as the Wave, which we boarded early Sunday morning (the 6th), and it required less than a half hour to land us at our destination. Our party consisted of our host and hostess and their daughter, Cora B. Green; Mr. B. F. Vandegrift, his wife, three daughters and son; James W. Shirley, wife, and two small children.

During the afternoon we were threatened with a rain-storm, and our party divided, some going into the caves for shelter, others repaired to a farm-house near by. The rain passed around us, after which a party of five in number, namely, Mr. and Mrs. Green, Mr. and Mrs. Vandegrift, and myself, reassembled on the summit of the elevation overlooking the Split Rock. It was suggested by me that we have a spirit seance, but we had no stand, slate or pencil. The novelty of a spirit seance on that noted spot was sufficiently suggestive and interesting to induce us to improvise a seat for the medium, which consisted of a couple of stakes driven into the ground and a fence rail placed on them. I took out my annotation book and with lead pencil placed it on Mrs. G.'s lap, and she threw over them a rubber circular, making the necessary condition of darkness. We formed a semi-circle in front of the medium thus seated, and sang the "Sweet Bye and Bye," and "Nearer My God to Thee." In a few moments the covering over the writing material was raised up and down three times, indicating thereby that the writing had been accomplished. In this way we received in rapid succession three communications, which I hereby transcribe and number them in the order of their production.

Number One.

"Good afternoon. Nice picnic. Many spirits with you, including Madam Ehrenborg and Swedenborg. Nettie, Emil, and Ida send much love to Mr. Helleberg and Mr. Stebbins."

Number Two.

"Mr. and Mrs. Vandegrift's friends send their greetings from summer land. Also, Mr. Green's friends and relatives. All happy to be with you."

Number Three.

"God bless you all, and hope we may all meet on this spot again. Good bye.

"Nettie and Curry."

We were not only delighted but enthusiastic over the success of our enterprise. Here on this spot, both romantic and famous in history, with illy-provided conditions, we had communed with the loved ones from the land of immortal souls.

As the spirit daughter of Mr. and Mrs. Stebbins, of Cincinnati, Ohio, is mentioned as belonging to the party of tourists that visited the planet Mars, and as communicating with others at Split Rock, Kentucky, and for other good reasons, I have deemed it not inappropriate to incorporate herein a letter of Mr. Stebbins to the *Spiritual Offering*, a paper recently established at Ottumwa, Iowa, and which is ably conducted and devoted to the advancement of spiritualism.

INDEPENDENT SLATE WRITING,

BY

EDWIN STEBBINS.

On Christmas evening myself and wife secured an independent slate-writing sitting with Mrs. Lizzie S. Green, at 309 Longworth street, Cincinnati, Ohio, and we received the following communication from our dear spirit daughter, viz:

"Merry, merry Christmas to you all! I do not know of a better Christmas gift than to give you a spirit communication on this memorable day. I am so happy and excited I can not write good. Oh, I have a beautiful home and am advancing in music all the time. I have a beautiful library of books. I am a teacher, and have a nice little class. We do not have as many scholars here in the spirit world as you do. We can not teach every one like we did here. We have to be attracted to each other magnetically. Therefore our work is not in vain, for by this method spiritual growth must ensue. We work in harmony together, and nothing occurs to retard our progress in learning. You would be surprised, and I rather think you are now, even at my style of composition. If you could see me as I am here, and hear me talk, you would see how fast I have progressed. Oh, how happy I am in my spirit home, but my heaven is not there. It is with my dear pa and ma, but duty calls and I must obey. I have been made extremely happy by your obedience to my will and all will be well. Henney says this is quite new to him, but when he saw you and me at his funeral his happiness was beyond expression. When you laid away my form of clay you did not think to see me here to talk and write to my loved ones dear.

"When you're sad and sometimes cry,
Remember your Ida, dear, is nigh,
To bless and comfort you while here,
And guide you to a brighter sphere.

"And when the time comes for you to go we will meet you with our golden boat, and row you safely over the beautiful river to our home that I have helped prepare for you. Now, thanking Mrs. Green for her kindness to you and Ida, I bid you good night. All the relatives are here, and send you their Christmas greetings.

"Good night, good night, to all that's here,
I leave and go to a brighter sphere.

Wishing you all success in the new year, dear pa and ma, ever hold sacred the Christmas gift I present you to-day. Good night, Mr. Green, wife and daughter. Good night, my dear pa and ma.

This indeed is the happiest Christmas I have spent since I left my earthly home. I must leave, but it is hard. Your loving daughter,

"Ida."

"My daughter passed away on the 18th day of December, 1875, at the age of seventeen, and she was an only child. The above message from her possesses peculiar value to me, for therein are a number of valuable tests and evidences of her identity. My belief in the return of the spirits of the departed is of brief duration in point of time antecedent, and was mainly brought about, through the mediumship of Mrs. Green. I can not express the real happiness I enjoy since I have been the recipient of this new light divine and I can only say, 'God speed the good work.'

"Cincinnati, Ohio."

ANNIE WINTERBURN.

"*Dear Brother*: Oh, how happy I am to-day to be able to write you on the inner surface of a double slate with your own precious hands holding it with the medium. You did not need this as a test, for your mind is clear and your heart is in the cause, but we give it to you because others have been thus favored, and we have resolved that you shall not be neglected when the good things pertaining to spirit intercourse are being given to others. Oh, John, you do give us so much real happiness by your noble and upright conduct, and by the opportunities you give us to hold sweet communion with you. Thus our lives become interblended, and the happiness of all increased. Spirits do derive great benefit from mortals, and to that extent are dependent on them. When a child dies in the tender years of infancy unschooled in the multifarious concernments of mortal life, it is brought back into contact with human affairs that it may learn those experiences of earth which were denied it by its early and untimely departure from the form. In all the pursuits of your life each individual is constantly attended by spirits interested in the same, and in these and many other ways are spirits aided in their progress and happiness. Whenever and by whomsoever you are told differently heed it not, but rely on what I have stated. We are interested in your proper instruction, and we will not lead you astray or into error. All those near and dear to you are here, and bid me to send you their love greetings. They pray without ceasing that you may be kept steady and firm in your high resolves and noble purposes until the end, when you shall rejoice in the anthem of victory. Hold up your head, dear and precious brother; be brave and resolute in the hour of temptation. Do no harm, but all the good you can in the world. And when the blessed angel called Death shall beckon you away from the labors and vicissitudes of mortal life to the sunlit evergreen shores of the summer land, be assured that among the hosts of others who will meet and welcome you with happy and rejoicing hearts you will see and be enfolded lovingly in the arms of your loving sister,

"Annie."

"I, John Winterburn, resident of Cincinnati, Ohio, do hereby certify that the above and foregoing communication from my spirit sister came in the manner, to wit: I examined a double slate, and found it clean and without any writing whatever upon it. A small piece of slate pencil not larger than a grain of wheat was placed upon it and the slate closed. I then held on to one side of the slate, holding it tight together as folded, and the medium, Mrs. Green, held on to the other side. Soon we heard writing, and in the course of fifteen minutes the signal was given indicating that the writing was completed, whereupon the slate was opened, and on both sides of the inner surfaces was found, neatly written, the above communication. The t's were crossed, and the i's were dotted. I know, as well as I am capable of knowing any fact requiring the exercise of my senses in their normal state, that the communication was written by invisible power, and I firmly believe it comes from the source it purports to come, namely: my dear sister, now in spirit life. The seance was in broad daylight, and under circumstances that precluded fraud or deception on the part of the medium or any one else in the body.

"John Winterburn, 185 Longworth street."

"This same Mr. Winterburn has had regularly one sitting a week with Mrs. Green for seven or eight months, and among other spirit relatives and friends who were active in communicating with him was his spirit sister Annie. She seems to possess considerable poetic ability, and occasionally wrote poetry to her brother. Recently Mr. Winterburn visited his mother country, England, and the last sitting with Mrs. G. before his departure, his sister Annie addressed the medium in the following feeling stanzas, which Mr. Winterburn copied as they came on the slate, viz:

"Dear medium friend, both good and true,
'Tis hard that we must part from you,
And though we cross the surging main,
We will return to you again.

"Returning with our spirits' love and power
From British isle or sunlit bower,
Our fond hearts' loving blessings to impart
To comfort and cheer your noble heart.

"Dear brother's heart you have made glad,
Dispersing sorrow and conditions sad;
And where'er we roam, on land or sea,
Our hearts shall turn in love to thee.

"Farewell, dear medium friend, farewell,
 To thee our gratitude we ne'er can tell,
We can only say heart's full of love,

We'll meet you on the shores above.

"And there, in that bright land of joy,
Where mingles naught of earth's alloy,
We'll lead thy steps with blessings rare
To our homes above our joys to share.

"Angels of light, refulgent bright,
Be with you when you take you flight
From scenes of strife and sorrows here
To a just reward in a higher sphere.

"Farewell, farewell, alas! farewell,
The parting is like a funereal knell;
But when you climb the golden stair,
Your true friend, Annie, will meet you there."

CHAPTER XXIII.

A SPIRIT PEELS A BANANA, AND EATS SOME OF IT, AND DIVIDES THE REST IN FOUR EQUAL PARTS—REPORTS OF CINCINNATI ENQUIRER ABOUT SPIRIT SEANCES AT MRS. GREEN'S.

I desire to speak of a recent manifestation, which baffles my ability to understand, and proves that spirits by some chemical process are enabled to operate upon material substances and cause them to vanish. I only give one instance, and leave the reader to his own reflections and to adopt his own theory. I shall simply give the fact as it occurred.

I have a little grand daughter, Julia Muth, in the spirit world. When in the form she was partially fond of bananas. On the occasion of the recent anniversary of her eighth birthday, the 13th of July, 1882, I went to Mrs. Green for a seance, taking with me a large banana. These slate-writing seances, as has been heretofore explained, take place in the full light. I sat, as usual, opposite to Mrs. Green, with the small stand between us. I placed the fruit on a slate, with a short letter of greeting, and put it under the covering of the stand, while Mrs. Green held another slate of her own. The spirits, after writing on Mrs. Green's slate for about an hour, wrote as follows: "Grandpa, take your slate from under the stand," which I immediately did, and on the slate was written, "I peeled the banana, and ate some of it, too; your little Julia Muth."

We removed the cloth covering from the stand and found the peelings on the floor, and on my slate the banana divided in four equal parts after the end piece had disappeared. We searched diligently, but without our effort being rewarded by the discovery of the missing portion of the fruit. Whither had it gone?

The *Cincinnati Daily Enquirer* is a leading as well as an extensively circulated paper, published at Cincinnati, Ohio, and, in October, 1881, Mrs. Green was visited by a reporter of that paper, who was present at two of her trumpet seances. Although probably not a believer, he turned out to be a fair minded man who would not allow his prejudices, if he had any, to interfere with an honest account of what he saw and witnessed. In three issues of that paper, to wit, October 16th, 18th and 21st, 1881, appeared his report of a visit to Mrs. Green, and two seances he attended. They are here inserted, in the order of the dates given.

Issue of October 16th:

"In a neatly furnished suit of rooms over No. 309 Longworth street lives Mrs. L. S. Green, a spiritualist medium. Upon her last evening a representative of the *Enquirer* called. He was cordially received by the lady's husband, being tendered a seat in a parlor in which was a piano, a pretty set of furniture; while an old-fashioned kerosene lamp threw its brightest rays over the room from a mantel-piece. Seated in a rocking-chair was Mrs. Green, plainly dressed, of a modest and retiring disposition, and features that stamped her as a faithful and loving wife. The mission of the newspaper man was quickly explained. Her husband replied that as a rule mediums avoided reporters, as they were liable to distort and ridicule their statements. But where the thing is conducted honestly and openly, 'I can not,' he said, 'see what we have to fear from publication.'

"In reply to a question, Mrs. Green said that she was about thirty-eight years old, and had been a clairvoyant since 1868, her first mediumistic inclinations having developed that year. Her history since that time as a spiritualist has been quite full of interest. Previous to her becoming a medium she was a member of the Christian Church, and was as great a skeptic as one could find. So, in fact, was her husband. While a member of the Indiana Legislature in 1867 he attended a seance, where he received a message from his dead mother. At a subsequent one, another spiritual letter came to him, telling him that his wife possessed the powers of a medium, and asking him to bring her to one of the circles. After some persuasion he finally gained her consent to go. She there saw her first spirits, that of an uncle of the medium of the assemblage, who had his head cut off by a train of cars. From that time her powers began to develop, showing themselves in messages that she wrote on paper or beheld in the air. Spirits as high as five hundred a day presented themselves to her view. Her continued increase as a medium so worked upon her that she lost her health, and she was compelled for the time being to abandon the business. About twelve months ago she resumed her writing—this time on slates. Messages Were written on the inside of folded slates, and often, after a seance, a fluid would be found on the outside of the slate, which, unless washed off then, could never be removed. This had been taken to chemist after chemist for analysis, and one and all had failed to make any thing out of it.

"One evening a small lock of hair was found in the corner of the slate, in the center of which was a small lead pencil. At that time this was believed to have been placed there by some one in the circle. It was folded in a piece of paper to be retained, but the next day it disappeared. From this time out Mrs. Green's materializing abilities began. She had great success in her seances, and frequently described catastrophes which, on the following morning, were found to be exceedingly accurate. She foreshadowed the explosion of the steamer Pat Rogers, and graphically described the collision of the United States with the America. The details of a fire at a neighboring place one evening were recited by her. The next day it was learned that the hour and facts were most wonderfully correct.

"While the reporter and his friend were talking Mrs. Green called their attention to two spirits who were standing besides them, one a brother-in-law of the first-named, and the other a friend of the latter who died twelve years ago. Both were accurately described, much to the surprise and astonishment of the two skeptics. Mrs. Green, in explaining her power, said that she was entirely controlled by one spirit, and that when she first began to work it was shown by slaps on the hand, by shocks in her arms, etc. She did only as her influence compelled her to act, and while writing, etc., she knew not what she did, much to the surprise and astonishment of the two skeptics. Many startling results of seances were recited, such as the sounding of trumpets, the ringing of bells, singing, and the appearance of different spirits were detailed."

Insertion of October 18th:

"Mrs. L. S. Green, the medium, gave a seance last evening to a few friends at her house, No. 309 Longworth street. There were five people present, three of whom were skeptics of the worst kind. The gathering was seated in a medium-sized; plainly-furnished room. In the center was a small stand, over which was placed a heavy green spread. As an opening, the lady took a small slate upon which was laid a bit of slate pencil. This she held with one hand in under the table, and several messages were written on it in a clear and distinct hand. Then the cloth was removed, and on the table were placed a bell, two slates, washed clean, a glass of water, and a leather trumpet. At some distance from the medium stood a guitar, leaning against the wall, and a large trumpet, while near the newspaper man were two small trumpets. The light was then extinguished, the doors locked, and the seance begun. All took hold of hands, and one of the party sang. In a few minutes came a gentle tapping on the slates, then the bell rang violently, seeming to pass through air, returning and falling on the floor. The various members were touched about the face and body, and one exceedingly lady-like spirit took occasion to rub her hand down the reporter's face, testing fully the power of his nervous system. Singing was continued, when the guitar was heard to play, rising in the air, apparently passing around over the different persons' heads, hitting them lightly in the face, and finally landing in the reportorial lap.

"A breathing spell was taken when one of the party varied the programme with a selection upon the orgamina. The favorite old song, 'John Brown,' was given, and it pleased the spirits hugely, as a deep bass voice was heard to join in with an occasional blast from the trumpet. Then the trumpet took a trip around the circle, announcing its coming with a rap on the head or shoulders of each one. The bell rose in the air tingling rapidly and landed this time on the table. The familiar taps on the person were continued, then there was a tremendous note from the trumpet, and a sweet voice joined in with Mrs. Green, as she sang, 'Nearer My God to Thee.' Although the manifestations were quite good, especially to the reporter, who was continually dodging imaginary trumpets and blows, the medium said the weather was bad for the most satisfactory work. The spirits announced that they were about ready to depart by a loud rap on the table and a sprinkling of those present with water. The light being turned on, the following communication was found on one of the slates:

"'Good evening, gentlemen. We are glad to meet you. The spirit band of the medium authorize and request me to thank the representative of that great metropolitan journal, the *Enquirer*, for the terms employed in reference to their medium and her gifts in yesterday's issue of that paper. This treatment, so rare, betokens a spirit of candor and fairness commensurate with this transcendently important subject. We extend you a cordial invitation to visit us whenever and as often as it suits your convenience, and we shall always endeavor to treat you with courtesy and respect.

"'Nettie.'

"The lines were very regular, the i's and t's are dotted, and the signature was especially plain, it being the name of one of Mrs. Green's controls."

The third and last appeared in the issue of October 21st, and is as follows:

"QUITE INTERESTING—A SEANCE HELD LAST EVENING—SKEPTICS AND BELIEVERS ASSEMBLE TOGETHER.

"A very interesting seance was held last evening at the residence of Mrs. L. S. Green, 309 Longworth street. Seven persons were present, including two mediums. The spirits were unusually frisky, and the manifestations were particularly gratifying to the believers, and rather dumbfounding to the skeptics. The arrangements and room were the same as in the others previously described, except that there were more musicians present. Very excellent music was rendered by an orgamina, a violin, a guitar, and a music-box. The selections given were sweet enough to summon the most bashful friends of the medium from their spiritualistic retreat. The departed were less inclined to epistolary efforts, and slate-writing was not conducted with any favorable results.

"During the evening one of the gentlemen sang a Swedish song, accompanying himself on the guitar. A female voice at one time, and a powerful bass later, were heard plainly in concert with him. The human singer alleged quite emphatically that his spiritual aids rendered the air in the same language he did. The guitar took numerous trips around the room, sometimes high in the air, again touching those present on the head and different parts of the body. A huge tin trumpet was blown most furiously, the blast sounding like the greatest effort of the bass-horn. Then it was pounded and thumped, creating a most awful din. This was explained as being the doings of a very powerfully materialized spirit. The statement was acquiesced in by a skeptic, who received a vigorous whack on the knee, fully convincing him that muscle, lots of it, too, backed the trumpet.

"A little music-box was taken from the table and wafted through the room, playing its peculiarly sweet airs all the time as it sailed toward the ceiling and over those about the table. It could be heard in every corner, high and low, and if a medium or friend was carrying it, said person must have been exceedingly lively, climbing over chairs, a bed, etc., without making any noise. It was claimed that when the box ran down it was wound up by those who took it through the air.

"Whenever songs were sung, or selections were played upon the instruments, soprano or bass voices joined in plain to all present. Members were delicately touched in the face and body. The tolling of a great bell was most cleverly imitated, and a little one was rung frequently. The spirits of loved ones were reported as standing at the sides of different members, some of whom were quickly recognized by the description given. Water was sprinkled on all, and the goblet filled with this fluid was passed around, touching some in the face, others on the body. No communications were received except very brief ones."

CHAPTER XXIV.

EXTRACTS FROM EACH OF TWO FUNERAL DISCOURSES BY BISHOP SIMPSON AND REV. W. H. THOMAS, D. D., WITH CONCLUSIONS OF C. G. HELLEBERG.

In closing it has been deemed advisable and proper to append an extract from each of two funeral discourses delivered by two eminent divines—one the eminent Methodist Bishop, Mr. Simpson, and the other a distinguished minister of Chicago, who, of late, experienced some little annoyance from his flock, who were mere sticklers for forms and creeds, and because their shepherd had grown a little beyond their cramped and narrow limits.

BISHOP SIMPSON.

"The very grave itself is a passage into the beautiful and glorious. We have laid our friends in the grave, but they are around us. The little children that sat upon our knee, into whose eyes we looked with love, whose little hands have clasped our neck, on whose cheek we have imprinted the kiss, we can almost feel the throbbing of their hearts to-day. They have passed from us, but where are they? Just beyond the line of the invisible. And the fathers and mothers who educated us, that directed and comforted us, where are they but just beyond the line of the invisible? The associates of our lives that walked along life's pathway, those with whom we took sweet counsel and who dropped from our side, where are they but just beyond us? not far away; but now it may be very near us. Is there any thing to alarm us in this thought? No. It seems to me that sometimes when my head is on the pillow there come whispers as of joy that drop into my heart—thoughts of the sublime and beautiful and glorious, as though some angel's wing passed over my brow, and some dear one sat by my pillow and communed with my heart to raise my affections to the other and better world. The invisible is not dark, it is glorious. Sometimes the veil becomes so thin it seems to me that I can almost see the bright forms through it, and my bending ear can almost hear the voices of those who are singing their melodious strains. Oh, there is music all around us, though in the busy scenes of life we recognize it not. The veil of the future will soon be lifted and the invisible shall appear."

REV. W. H. THOMAS, D. D., OF CHICAGO.

"How can we linger over the bier of the departed and go in the eventide to their graves, and sit down in the stillness there, hoping in some way to come in communion with them. They carry their loves over to the other side, and is it unreasonable to suppose that a mother who has passed from these shores should still seek to be the guardian angel of the children she watched over in this life? Is it unreasonable that the great hosts of life, column on column, world on world, that have gone out from this state, should seek to come with their higher wisdom and tenderer sympathy to minister to those they loved in this life, and help them to cling to the truth that saves? To me this doctrine of the spirit life, the eminence and presence of helping and guiding spirits is a comforting thought. It brings me into the presence of the innumerable host that people the spirit land. It gives me somehow a consciousness of the great fact of immortality. It gives me a sweet consciousness that my friends live on the other shore; that to me they will come as ministering angels in the dying hour to receive the spirit, tired by work, weakened by sickness, wearied with years, pale from death, and bear it to the love and life above."

If these utterances are not in harmony with spiritualism, and its central and prominent idea of the very nearness of our spirit friends and the spirit world, then I am wholly incapable of recognizing and understanding the force of plain and direct language. They can have but one meaning, and that in perfect accordance with spiritualism.

I find these extracts published in the Auburn *Advertiser*, of New York, from which I copied them. There they are; read them carefully, and then propound the question to your own heart and intelligence, namely: What does all this mean if spiritualism be false? And if spiritualism be true, how can these men and those holding similar views, oppose spiritualism and be consistent and maintain their self-respect?

C. G. Helleberg.

www.ingramcontent.com/pod-product-compliance
Lightning Source LLC
Chambersburg PA
CBHW060513090426
42735CB00011B/2200